CARING FOR CANADIANS

Caring for Canadians
in a Canada Strong and Free

Mike Harris & Preston Manning

THE FRASER INSTITUTE

Institut économique
de Montréal

2005

Series editor: Fred McMahon
Volume editor: Nadeem Esmail
Director of Publication Production: Kristin McCahon

Editorial assistance provided by White Dog Creative Inc.
Cover design by Brian Creswick @ GoggleBox
Coordination of French publication: Martin Masse

Date of issue: October 2005
Printed and bound in Canada

Library and Archives Canada Cataloguing in Publication Data

Harris, Mike, 1945-
    Caring for Canadians in a Canada strong and free / Mike Harris & Preston Manning

Issued also in French under title: Au service des Canadiens dans un Canada fort et prospère.
Co-published by Institut économique de Montréal.
Includes bibliographical references.
ISBN 0–88975–226–5

    1. Canada--Social policy.   2. Medical policy--Canada.   3. Child care--Government policy--Canada.   4. Education and state--Canada.   5. Public welfare--Canada   I. Manning, Preston, 1942-   II. Fraser Institute (Vancouver, B.C.)   III. Institut économique de Montréal   IV. Title.

HV108.H38 2005   361.6´1´097109051   C2005-906053-0

CONTENTS

MIKE HARRIS

Mike Harris was born in Toronto in 1945 and raised in Callander and North Bay, Ontario. Prior to his election to the Ontario Legislature in 1981, Mike Harris was a schoolteacher, a School Board Trustee and Chair, and an entrepreneur in the Nipissing area.

On June 8, 1995, Mike Harris became the twenty-second Premier of Ontario following a landslide election victory. Four years later, the voters of Ontario re-elected Mike Harris and his team, making him the first Ontario Premier in more than 30 years to form a second consecutive majority government.

After leaving office, Mr. Harris joined the law firm of Goodmans LLP as a Senior Business Advisor and acts as a consultant to various Canadian companies. Mr. Harris serves as a Director on several corporate Boards including Magna International and Canaccord Capital Inc. and is Board Chair of the Chartwell Seniors Housing REIT. He also serves on a number of corporate Advisory Boards for companies such as Aecon and Marsh Canada. Mr. Harris also serves as a Director on the Boards of the Tim Horton Children's Foundation and the St. John's Rehabilitation Hospital.

He is also a Senior Fellow of The Fraser Institute, a leading Canadian economic, social research, and education organization.

PRESTON MANNING

Preston Manning served as a Member of the Canadian Parliament from 1993 to 2001. He founded two new political parties—the Reform Party of Canada and the Canadian Reform Conservative Alliance—both of which became the Official Opposition in the Canadian Parliament. Mr. Manning served as Leader of the Opposition from 1997 to 2000 and was also his party's critic for Science and Technology.

Since retirement from Parliament in 2002, Mr. Manning has released a book entitled *Think Big* (published by McClelland & Stewart) describing his use of the tools and institutions of democracy to change Canada's national agenda. He has also served as a Senior Fellow of the Canada West Foundation and as a Distiguished Visitor at the University of Calgary and the University of Toronto. He is currently a Senior Fellow of The Fraser Institute and President of the Manning Centre for Building Democracy.

Mr. Manning continues to write, speak, and teach on such subjects as the revitalization of democracy in the Western world, relations between Canada and the United States, strengthening relations between the scientific and political communities, the development of North American transportation infrastructure, the revitalization of Canadian federalism, the regulation of the genetic revolution, and the management of the interface between faith and politics.

ACKNOWLEDGMENTS

We have a number of people to thank. Former Fraser Institute Executive Director, Michael Walker, and the current Executive Director, Mark Mullins, were instrumental in initiating this project and guiding it. Fred McMahon and Nadeem Esmail of The Fraser Institute played key roles in coordinating the research effort that stands behind the policies presented here. Michel Kelly-Gagnon, president of the Montreal Economic Institute, generously lent us his considerable expertise. We owe a debt of gratitude to many Fraser Institute research analysts, in particular, Jason Clemens, Niels Veldhuis, Claudia Hepburn, and Sylvia LeRoy, for their hard work in providing the data we requested.

We are grateful for Kristin McCahon's steering of this project through the production process. Martin Masse of the Montreal Economic Institute did heroic work managing the translation on a tight deadline. Both Jean Marie Clemenger, Preston Manning's secretary and researcher, and Elaine Pritchard, Mike Harris's assistant, did exemplary work in keeping the project on track.

Of course, we take full responsibility for the ideas and interpretations presented here. While we have relied on the insights of many, we set the analysis and the policy choices this document reflects.

FOREWORD

In March of this year, under the auspices of The Fraser Institute, we published a report entitled *A Canada Strong and Free*. We began with positive recollections of the great things Canadians have achieved together in the past. But we also asked: What now of the future? Where is that strong clear national vision that will unite and guide Canada for the twenty-first century? And what are the public policies that will make that future a reality?

In recent months the strains on the unity of our country have increased, due to fiscal imbalances between the federal and provincial governments, the revitalization of separatist sentiment in Quebec, and the growing estrangement of Western Canada from Ottawa. Where is the national vision and policies that will transcend and alleviate these strains?

Under normal circumstances, Canadians would look to their federal political leaders and parties to answer such questions. But these are confusing and disquieting times in our national politics. The revelations of the Gomery Inquiry, the machinations and indecisiveness of a minority parliament, constant attacks on the trustworthiness of national party leaders—all have undermined many Canadians' confidence in national parties, parliament, elections, politics, even in democracy itself. A "vision deficit" and a "policy deficit" have emerged, which the up-coming federal election is unlikely to remedy.

To address these twin deficits, we proposed in our first report that Canadians envision a future in which we "strive to achieve standards of living, economic performance, and democratic governance that are the highest in the world and enable Canada to be a model of international leadership and citizenship." We proposed that policies to realize this vision be based on the principles of real democracy, freedom of choice, acceptance of personal responsibility and "rebalanced federalism."

We illustrated how these principles might be applied in practice, discussing their application to health-care reform, improved economic performance, optimizing the size of government, eliminating Canada's "democratic deficit" and advancing our national interests on the world stage. We also tapped data from a national public opinion survey to assess the feasibility of gaining public acceptance of policies based on such principles.

In this second volume of the Canada Strong and Free series, we want to return to the first component of our national vision—enabling Canadians to achieve the highest quality of life in the world. While quality of life means different things to different people, in this volume we have focused on how our principles of freedom of choice, acceptance of personal responsibility, and rebalanced federalism can dramatically improve the provision of education, welfare, health care, and child care in Canada.

In particular, the principle of rebalanced federalism would clearly allocate responsibility for the services most essential to the quality of individuals' lives—education, social assistance, and health—along with the appropriate taxing authority, to the levels of government closest to the people served.

Words such as "vision," "principles," and "policies" are useful abstractions that help us analyze public problems and propose solutions. But for individual Canadians and communities, "quality of life" is not an abstraction. It represents the personal well-being of real human beings and their families. Poverty, the despair of the welfare trap, illness and the anxiety of the waiting-list for care (or even diagnosis), the natural need of children for security and their requirements of knowledge and skill to succeed in an ever-changing world, these are not abstractions either. They are the daily experience of millions of Canadians—conditions that must be changed and needs that must be met, if our policy proposals are to make a real difference to the quality of our fellow citizens' lives.

The viability and acceptability of our proposals should therefore be judged not merely from an intellectual or ideological standpoint. They must be assessed on the basis of whether, at the end of the day, their implementation would significantly improve the daily lives and personal futures of individual Canadians and their families in thousands of communities across our country.

It is with this end in view that we invite you to examine the policy proposals in this volume.

Mike Harris
Toronto, Ontario

Preston Manning
Calgary, Alberta

EXECUTIVE SUMMARY

GOAL To give Canadians the highest quality of life in the world.

FOCUS This volume focuses on public policies to dramatically improve Canada's approach to K-12 education, welfare, health care, and child care. It addresses the questions of how to structure federal/provincial health care relations in light of the Supreme Court's *Chaoulli* decision, and how to relieve the growing federal/provincial tensions in other social service areas that threaten national unity.

PRINCIPLES

* Federal respect for provincial jurisdiction.

* Services to be provided wherever possible by levels of government and delivery organizations closest to those they serve.

* Maximization of freedom of choice for service recipients and acceptance of greater responsibility for choices and personal well-being.

CURRENT APPLICATION OF PRINCIPLES

Federal respect for provincial jurisdiction, and increased freedom of choice, are most pronounced with respect to K-12 education. After going in the opposite direction for many years, these principles are now increasingly being applied with good results in the field of public welfare. Although in the past these principles have been totally disregarded with respect to the provision of health care, there are hopeful signs (*Chaoulli* decision of

Supreme Court) that Canadians are beginning to consider other alternatives. With respect to the federal role in child care, Canada is still going down the wrong road.

SPECIFIC RECOMMENDATIONS

K-12 EDUCATION

* Continued federal respect for provincial jurisdiction in K-12 education.

* Parents not using public education should be provided a voucher worth 50% of the total per-student cost of education at a public school for other forms of education, whether private school, at-home schooling, or other.

* Families with children with special needs should be provided a voucher worth 75% of the total cost of their child's education in the public system so they can enroll in school that meets their children's unique needs

* All K-12 schools should be held accountable for results and given freedom to innovate.

WELFARE

* Ottawa should continue to devolve responsibility and increasingly provide no-strings-attached funding to the provinces, vacating the appropriate amount of tax room to fully respect provincial responsibility in this area.

* Provinces should pursue policies that:
  * Encourage work.
  * Make work pay by structuring welfare so that those who enter the workforce are better off.
  * Set timelines for recipients to enter the workforce.
  * Help potential recipients before they enter the welfare rolls.
  * Establish a separate program for the disabled to provide long-term help that recognizes their special needs and allows them to live a life of dignity.

HEALTH CARE

* Commit Canada to the goal of achieving the best health care in the world by providing universal access regardless of ability to pay, but offering a "mixed approach" (public and private) to delivery, payment, and health care insurance.

* End federal transfers and vacate the appropriate amount of tax room for the provinces.

* Provincial governments should:
    * Right size health ministries; have them fund and regulate but not supply health services.
    * Increase the accountability of health care providers and provide more independent information on outcomes so that patients can make informed decisions.
    * Form partnerships with the private sector to provide services and infrastructure more efficiently.
    * Pay health care providers for the services they provide.
    * Empower Canadians to make their own decisions about health care.

CHILD CARE

* Reverse the current direction of increasing federal involvement in pre-scribing and funding child-care options.

* End federal transfers and vacate the appropriate amount of tax room for the provinces.

* Stop favouring one form of childcare over another by the use of biased tax breaks that often favour affluent two income families over those who choose to parent at home.

* Provide support for self-employed parents as well as employed parents to parent at home.

1 EDUCATING FUTURE GENERATIONS

EDUCATION POLICY IN CANADA

We envision a future in which every Canadian child enjoys the best educational opportunities on Earth, one in which Canada's youth lead the world in international comparisons of knowledge, skills and achievement.

The reality, we are glad to report, is much brighter here than in any other policy realm we examine in this series. Canada can be proud of its educational achievement.

This is, in our view, hardly surprising. As we shall see, education is the only one of the four policy areas this document addresses in which our principle of a balanced federalism is completely respected. In this field alone, do the provinces maintain effective control of their own choices.

Likewise, we find it profoundly telling that the good results are most striking in those provinces that have emphasized our other guiding principles of personal choice and responsibility. The provinces that have followed this route—Alberta, British Columbia, Manitoba, and Quebec—lead the rest in educational achievement. Alberta, which has gone furthest to encourage choice and responsibility, is a world leader.

THE NEED: PREPARING OUR CHILDREN TO LEAD THE WORLD

It is a truism of the 21st-century economy that knowledge is the key to personal success. Canada's children deserve the world's best education. Canadian families deserve the help they need to provide it.

All children deserve a learning environment that nurtures their knowledge, skills, and personal growth, one that equips them to seize every opportunity their lives will present. No child should be trapped in a poorly performing school.

Each child is also unique and deserves a school that meets their particular needs, one that provides for the development of their individual gifts. Families should have help in accessing the educational environment that best meets the needs of their children.

Four provinces, Alberta, Quebec, British Columbia, and Manitoba, offer parents a portion of what it costs to educate their children in a public school so that they may, if they wish, choose another environment more suited to their children's particular needs. Those provinces have achieved world-class excellence in education, confirmed by international comparisons of educational achievement.

Six provinces deny school choice—except to families prosperous enough to afford it on their own. We are being unfair to those provinces' other families: the lack of choice clearly disadvantages poorer children. This is wrong. Canada should be a land of opportunity for rich and poor alike.

We believe that Canadian children from one coast to the other deserve the same opportunities that children enjoy in Quebec or Alberta. Canadians in every province, from Newfoundland to British Columbia, should have access to the best educational choices available in the world.

WHAT IS BEING DONE?
CREATIVE STUDIES

Canadians value education highly and appreciate the need for their children to gain a firm foundation of skills in their formative years. As a country, we reflect that in our education spending. Canada ranks well over the average in primary and secondary education spending per student, ranking seventh among the 21 OECD countries (OECD, 2001).

Yet spending does not determine the quality of the education system. One Canadian province, Alberta, is an undisputed world leader in educational achievement, not because its spending is unusually high, but because it allows freedom and choice. Others are not far behind: British

Columbia, Manitoba, and Quebec have attained excellence with transparent and accountable testing programs and curriculum-based school exit exams (Bishop, 1999). Children in these four provinces have won honours for their performance in national and international tests.

If we care for our children's future, we adults will learn lessons from their successes.

RESPECTING PROVINCIAL AUTONOMY

Under our Constitution, Canada's provinces have exclusive jurisdiction over education policy and funding. Almost uniquely, the federal government has not sought to interfere with this authority, as it has in so many other areas of provincial jurisdiction. Provinces are entirely free to design programs that suit the needs of their citizens.

Few other countries offer their component jurisdictions so much autonomy over education—or see a fraction of the diversity in the result. Our federal government provides no funding, imposes no curriculum, nor attempts any regulation of primary or secondary (K-12) education.[1] National initiatives in areas like testing and program coordination are developed solely by provincial authorities through the Council of Ministers of Education, Canada (CMEC).

This unusual level of freedom, coupled with the provinces' very different histories, founding populations, and cultures, has produced dramatically different education systems across Canada. Indeed, even the term "public education" does not mean the same thing in one province as it does in any other.

The results confirm the wisdom of this approach. In a recent study comparing 31 nations, Canadian students ranked second in reading, fifth in science, and sixth in mathematics (Bussière et al., 2004).

---

1   The portion of tuition at independent religious schools that is applicable to religious instruction is eligible for the standard federal income-tax credit for charitable donations.

Significantly, provinces that also follow our other guiding principles of freedom of choice and personal responsibility also do significantly better than provinces that disregard them.

THE ALBERTA EXAMPLE

Alberta, the country's top academic scorer, provides an example of how common-sense policies can produce an education system ranked among the best in the world. This is not due to huge spending on education. Indeed, Alberta spends less per capita on education than Newfoundland, spends roughly the same on education as Saskatchewan, and does not spend significantly more than most other provinces (figure 1). Instead, Alberta excels in Canadian and international comparisons because it enables families to choose the best educational alternatives for their children.

Not coincidentally, the province that leads the nation in scholastic achievement also ranked first in The Canadian Education Freedom Index

FIGURE 1: EDUCATION SPENDING PER CAPITA, 2003/2004

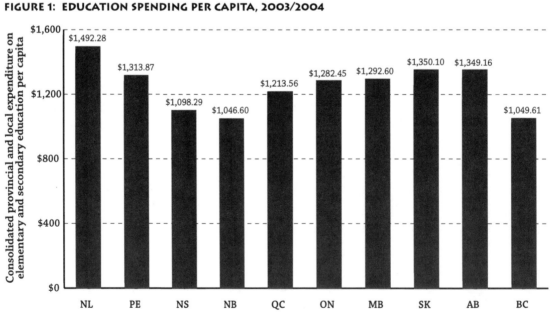

Source: Statistics Canada, Public Institutions Division, 2005.

(Hepburn and Van Belle, 2003). In the words of the United Nations Declaration of Human Rights, Alberta gives its parents more power, "to determine the kind of education that shall be given to their children."

Alberta has identified and implemented policies that international research and its own experience have proven to raise both standards and citizen satisfaction levels. These do not rely purely on either public or private delivery models but use the best in each to challenge and energize the system as a whole.

First, Alberta ensures equity and choice by funding education in independent schools and at home, as well as in the public system. Accredited private schools receive subsidies worth approximately 60% of the basic per-student grant available to public schools, or approximately 35% of the total cost of educating a student in the public system (about $2,500). Children with special education needs who attend private schools receive the same funding as they would if they were attending public schools. Accredited independent schools also receive public funding for supervising the education of home-schooled students, while the parents of those children may receive public funding equal to approximately 16% of what is spent to educate a child in the public system.

Thanks to sound public-policy decisions that encourage excellence and diversity—and defying some critics' apprehensions—Alberta's parents do not always decide that the best choice for their children lies outside the public system. To the contrary.

In 1994, when public funding for independent schools was increased, the government also made changes to encourage the public system to become more "goal-oriented, service-oriented, and responsive to market forces" (Bosetti, O"Reilly, and Gereluk, 1998: 2). School boards acquired more control over how they produced academic results, while becoming more accountable for those results. Other reforms included standardized testing, high school diploma exams, and "charter schools." These last, the only ones in Canada, empower communities to start schools that respond to a local educational need. Although run independently of local school boards, charter schools are public institutions that may neither charge tuition nor exclude any student.

In fact, charter schools have not gained a large foothold in Alberta. In part, that is because Edmonton's far-sighted school superintendent, Emery Dosdall, responded to demands from parents and educators for new programs by encouraging them to open as new schools under his own board. Today, Edmonton is home to more than 30 different educational programs at more than 140 locations. The board has rid itself of "catchment areas" and instead offers elementary students bus service to their family's choice of facility. Researchers found that in 2001 only 51% of Edmonton public school students attended their neighbourhood school—49% attended another Edmonton public school (Hepburn and Van Belle, unpublished).

Calgary was initially slower to provide choices and, over opposition from the local school board, became home to six charter schools.[2] But as choices multiplied in Edmonton, attracting international attention, the Calgary board began to change its stance. Between 2001 and 2004, that board opened 26 new programs or program locations. Though these choices still pale in comparison to Edmonton's, they are generous in comparison to much of the rest of Canada.

EDUCATIONAL FREEDOM IN OTHER PROVINCES

Alberta is not the only province that encourages equity and excellence through choice and accountability. British Columbia, Manitoba, and Quebec also provide some public funding for children attending independent schools. Like Alberta, these provinces allow the funding to be applied to operating costs and insist that the schools teach the provincial curriculum. Manitoba and Quebec allow funding for schools that operate for profit, which further increases parental choice.

Ontario flirted briefly with a refundable tax credit for parents of children at independent schools but currently provides no assistance for this choice. Saskatchewan and the Atlantic provinces offer no financial

---

2 Charter applicants in Alberta must first apply for status to their local school board. If the school board denies them a charter, they may appeal to the minister of education, as happened in all six cases in Calgary.

support for families that choose independent schools. Independent schools are also heavily regulated in these provinces, making it doubly difficult for them to provide parents with any real alternative to the public system. Tellingly, the same provinces tend to perform below the Canadian average on national and international tests (SAIP and PISA) (CMEC, 2005).

THE REPORT CARD ON CHOICE

Alberta gives parents the widest school choice in Canada. It also tops the provinces—and most of the world—in educational achievement. In the rankings on reading literacy, Alberta ranks not only ahead of all the other Canadian provinces, it ranks higher than any of the other 40 nations in the study save Finland (figure 2). In science, Alberta again ranks ahead of all the other provinces and is outscored only by Finland and Japan, while students in Hong Kong put in a performance equalling Alberta's (figure 3). In mathematics, Alberta again leads Canadian provinces, followed by British Columbia and Quebec. Only Hong Kong outranks Alberta (figure 4).

Along with Alberta, the provinces that encourage some parental choice or that have parents making choices despite a lack of support from the provincial government, rank above the others. In mathematics and science, students in Alberta, British Columbia, and Quebec outperformed the Canadian average and all other provinces. For reading, students in Alberta, British Columbia, and Ontario outperformed their counterparts in other provinces and the Canadian average for all students.

Canadians can lead the world in education. Canadians in those provinces that encourage choice tend to outperform their neighbours. Families across Canada deserve the excellence of educational opportunities found where parental choice is allowed.

Though most people agree that a choice of schools benefits children, some worry that government funding of independent schools may have negative consequences for the public system. We sometimes hear that such funding will result in "cream skimming," as the best teachers and brightest students abandon public schools, leaving them a sort of educational ghetto populated only by those who can't afford or access better private schools.

FIGURE 2: PISA SCORES FOR READING, 2003

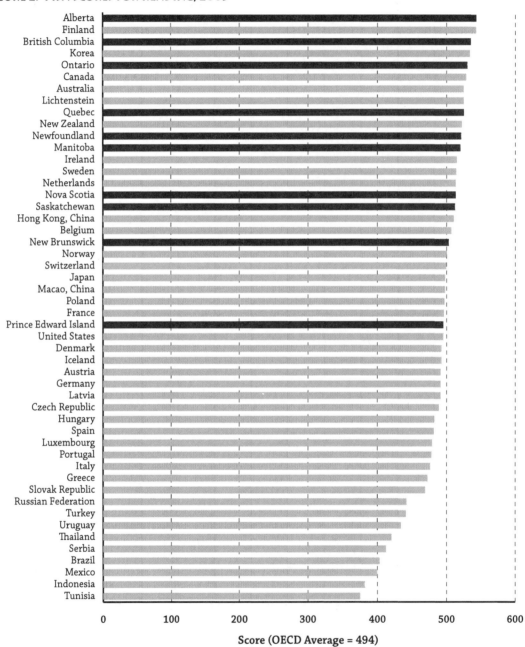

PISA = Programme for International Student Assessment, a project of the OECD. Source: Bussière et al., 2004.

FIGURE 3: PISA SCORES FOR SCIENCE, 2003

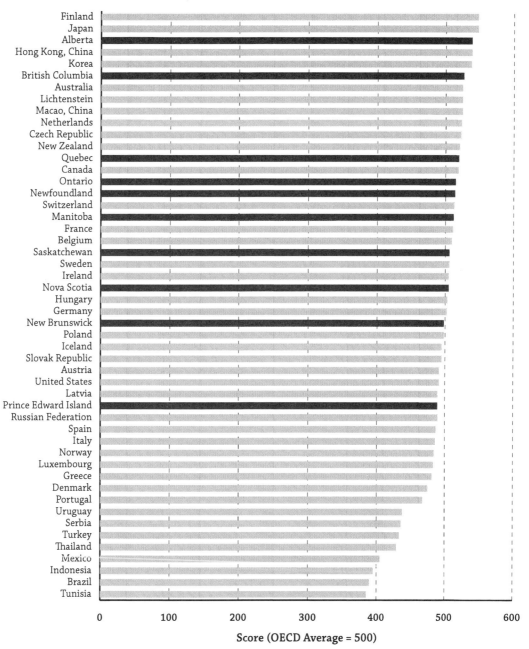

Score (OECD Average = 500)

PISA = Programme for International Student Assessment, a project of the OECD. Source: Bussière et al., 2004.

FIGURE 4: PISA SCORES FOR COMBINED MATHEMATICS, 2003

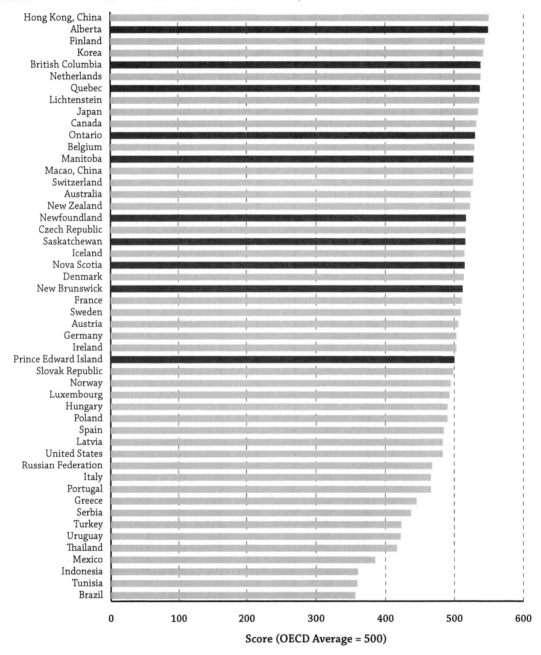

PISA = Programme for International Student Assessment, a project of the OECD. Source: Bussière et al., 2004.

International and Canadian evidence puts those fears to rest. When policies are well constructed, children in both systems wind up winners. The largest study ever done of educational efficiency, by Germany's Kiel Institute, reveals a powerful link between the health of private education and achievement in the public system. "International differences in student performance are not caused by differences in schooling resources but are mainly due to differences in educational institutions," the study concludes (Wößmann, 2000: Abstract). Competition from private schools inspires excellence among public schools.

Further evidence that private-school competition improves public-school performance comes from the United States. Noted Harvard economist Caroline M. Hoxby summarized the effect in this conclusion to one of her many studies of school choice:

> It appears that public schools are induced to raise achievement when they are faced with competition and that this effect swamps any effect associated with cream skimming, reverse cream skimming or the like. The choice reforms that are currently in place do not appear to generate winners and losers, but only winners. Public school students who are often predicted to be losers, are winners because their schools respond positively to competitive threats. This is not only good news for students; it should be welcome news to those who think that public schools have much good potential. (Hoxby, 2001: 22)

It is equally clear in Canada that public funding of private and home schools has resulted in neither a mass exodus from the public system nor a reduction in the quality of public education. Though independent school enrollment has increased in Alberta (as in most other provinces), it remains well below the national average (Statistics Canada, 2001). Astonishingly, it remains similar to Ontario, which provides no public support for independent schools and sends 22% of its students to separate Catholic schools (Hepburn and Van Belle, 2003: 20). Rather than encourage a rush to private schools, Alberta seems to have given families good cause to choose public education.

THE POSSIBILITIES: RAISING OUR MARKS

PRINCIPLES

Education is the one policy field discussed in these pages where the balance of Confederation is respected: provinces not only have the responsibility for education, they are free from federal interference. It should surprise no one that it is also the one area of social policy in which Canada clearly excels. Respecting the constitutional authority of provinces demonstrably produces superior results.

But we can do still better. The other fundamental principles we embrace—choice and personal responsibility—also provide guidance on how to increase our educational achievement.

Education is, at heart, a family matter. It may be subsidized by the state, guided by provincial curricula, and monitored by public inspectors but the responsibility for choosing the best education for each child lies with parents. Families across Canada deserve the excellence of educational opportunities found where parental choice is allowed. No child should be forced to attend a school that does not meet his or her needs. These choices should reside with families, providing them the means, freedom, and responsibility to choose the best education possible for their children. In their individual choices, they will also illuminate the path to national excellence in education.

Quality, accountability, and equity are three further common-sense objectives for Canadian education policy. Ministries of education must define their objectives, teach towards them, measure their success, and inform parents and the public of their results. They must also reach out not only to the average or most able students but to those with special needs or at risk of dropping out of school.

POLICY PROPOSALS

1 *Parents opting for independent education should receive a voucher worth 50% of the total per-student cost of public education.*

According to a Leger Marketing poll, 32% of Canadians are dissatisfied with their province's school system (Canadian Press/Leger Marketing, 2003). A voucher system for children up to age 18 would allow these parents to find more satisfactory solutions. Families would have the resources to take advantage of the growing number of education alternatives: full-day, part-time, or after-school community programs, or e-schooling via the internet. Needless to say, both parents and government have the responsibility to ensure that these alternatives are indeed educating children and are not engaged in any inappropriate or illegal activity.

2 *Support children with special needs whose parents choose alternative education by providing their families with a voucher worth 75% of the cost of their education in the public system.*

Children with special needs require special support. Although education systems across the country spend large sums on special-needs programs, parents are often dissatisfied with their results[3] and resort to home or independent schooling if they can afford them. Children with special needs cannot wait for the system to be fixed. It is only fair that their parents receive some additional help with the challenge of meeting their children's needs. Some provinces, including British Columbia, Alberta, and Manitoba, deserve credit for providing special funding for these students to attend independent schools.

3 *Hold all K-12 schools accountable for results, while giving them freedom to innovate.*

Provinces should encourage site-based management of public schools, giving principals control over budgets and staffing and holding them to account for their results. Market mechanisms can further increase public

---

3   See in particular the 2001 *Annual Report* of Ontario's Provincial Auditor on the failure of Ontario's public school system to serve special needs children adequately (Government of Ontario, 2001).

school accountability. Parents allowed to choose their children's schools will choose those that produce the best results. Money will follow students. Schools that succeed will prosper and grow.

WHAT WOULD THESE REFORMS MEAN FOR YOUR CHILDREN AND FOR YOU?

If these policy proposals were enacted, your choices for your child's education would multiply. With funding now available to educational entrepreneurs, you would see parents like yourselves band together with a few motivated teachers to start schools that respond to their children's particular needs and interests. You would see some schools designed to attract families concerned with the "three R's"; others that would respond to concerns for religious or social values. Since tuition would often be less than $4,000 per year, these new "private" schools would no longer be the preserve of the wealthy but attract the same mix of students from all income groups that we associate with the best public schools.

Doubtless some of your child's classmates would switch to those new schools. They would be the children whose parents have always been frustrated with the local public school but couldn't afford the move to another neighbourhood or the tuition for a private school; the kids being bullied; the pupils whose special needs haven't been met; perhaps even those whose parents you think have unrealistic expectations about what their school should be providing!

Meanwhile you would also see changes in the public system. Teachers would breathe a sigh of relief as they no longer had to cope with the impossible burden of being all things to all people. They would be able to concentrate on serving the families that really wanted their children to be there and who supported the job they were doing. Then they would set to work to make public schools even better to attract still more families.

As a parent, perhaps you would stay with the re-invigorated public system. Perhaps you would find a compelling appeal to one of the new independent schools. Either way, you would know you had choices, more and better ones than are currently available to you.

The biggest winners would be your children. Not necessarily those of wealthy families, who can already afford the best that independent schools have to offer, but those of parents who dream of a better life for their children than their own, knowing that nothing is more important to their future success than a good education. Your children will enter their early adulthood as the best educated, best prepared, young people in the world.

2 LENDING A HELPING HAND

WELFARE POLICY IN CANADA

We envision a more productive and prosperous Canada where all Canadians can build better lives for themselves and their families (this will be the subject of a future volume of our *Canada Strong and Free* series). We also envision a caring Canada, always ready to help those in need, to comfort and assist individuals and families when misfortune strikes, and offer them the opportunity to rebuild self-sufficient lives.

But what is the reality for too many Canadians? Over 1.7 million Canadians—5.4% of our fellow citizens—live on welfare. They find themselves trapped in poverty by social "assistance" programs that increase, rather than decrease, their state of dependence.

In our land of opportunity and wealth, this is an unacceptable sign that we are failing too many of our fellow Canadians. We believe Canada can do better.

THE NEED: PATHWAYS OUT OF WANT

We believe Canadians on welfare, or in danger of falling onto social assistance, need and deserve a strong helping hand. Compassion should be a guiding principle in welfare reform.

But compassion must go beyond a monthly cheque. Programs that leave individuals and families trapped in dependence are not compassionate. They are particularly damaging for children, who may come to believe that the doors of opportunity are closed to them.

Programs must be based on the best empirical evidence and carefully designed to help individuals and families begin building greater hope and prosperity for the future, to get on with productive, independent lives.

As with all government services financed by taxpayers, economy must also guide welfare reform. This is so not simply out of a desire to save money. High and increasing welfare spending is not an indicator of caring programs. It is a sign that we are failing; that those already on welfare remain trapped in dependency and that others are joining them. By contrast, programs that provide to Canadians in need the freedom and opportunity to take responsibility for their own lives, will by their very nature save money over time.

That said, a reduction in spending due merely to lower benefits is not, by itself, a sign of success. The sad reality is that too many Canadians are, in effect, warehoused in the welfare system—"out of sight, out of mind." They lack the help, advice, skills, motivation, and incentives they need to begin building new, more prosperous, lives for themselves and their families.

Beyond compassion and economy, the central principles guiding welfare reform must be freedom and responsibility, and the right division of responsibility between levels of government. We believe that individuals and families given the freedom to determine their own fate will look after themselves far better than any government program. In the same spirit, we believe that the government closest to the people it serves but still large enough to be able to raise sufficient funds will, given responsibility, resources, and freedom to innovate within a rebalanced federalism, best serve its citizens.

By far the best welfare "outcome" for most recipients is a job—paying work. We will propose in this section policies that have helped hundreds of thousands of Canadians find jobs and begin building hope and prosperity for themselves and their families.

It may seem obvious to say that those who escape the welfare-dependency trap by finding work should benefit from their efforts. Sadly, this is too often not the case. "Claw-backs" often leave them little better off or even worse off. Recipients who enter the workforce need to reap the rewards and see their standard of living increase. We propose to ensure that.

True success for Canadians on, or at risk of joining, welfare rolls lies in reducing their dependency, combined with real gains in earned income. That is our goal for welfare reform.

It is already being achieved in some Canadian provinces.

WHAT IS BEING DONE? LEARNING HOW TO HELP

The good news is that hundreds of thousands of Canadians have escaped the welfare trap in the last decade. As recently as 1994, over 3 million Canadians—*more than 10%* of our population—were on welfare. That number has been cut by nearly one-half in the last decade. How has this been achieved?

Innovative programs in a number of provinces are giving welfare recipients what they need to begin rebuilding their lives. Teamed-up with experienced workers who understand their plight, Canadians on welfare are now receiving the assistance and expertise they need to re-enter the workforce. Such programs also lend every effort to ensure that Canadians in need, but not yet dependent on welfare, find better alternatives.

Driving much of this change in policy over the last decade was concern over rising welfare dependency and budgetary deficits. From 1980 to 1994, the percentage of Canadians supported by social assistance nearly doubled: from 5.4% to 10.7%. Typically, welfare rolls expanded during bad times but then failed to shrink during good times. More and more Canadians became trapped in dependency. This growing dependency was reflected in the nation's fiscal burden. In 1980, spending on all social programs amounted to 14.3% of gross domestic product (GDP); by 1992, this figure had risen to 21.1% (Battle, 1998).

Far from reflecting a caring society, these increased costs were a sign of failure to help recipients renew lives and livelihoods. In effect, they were the price of a heartless willingness to warehouse needy Canadians in dependency.

In part because of this financial pressure, the provinces responded to varying degrees by reducing welfare benefits. In addition, many provinces tightened eligibility requirements, especially where government support was considered less important, as for single employables. As well, a number of provinces adopted anti-fraud measures. These are often criticized but can be essential to the success of overall reform: people who learn how to game the welfare system are motivated to remain on its support rather than seek independence from it.

Reducing the pressure on public spending also leads to other benefits. It frees resources to focus on those in greatest need and those moving from dependency to self-sufficiency. But welfare reform must go beyond saving money—or it will fail the very people it is intended to help. Fortunately, well-designed reforms have been shown to provide great benefits for those on assistance.

Most importantly, application of the principle of "rebalanced federalism" has enabled transformation in this important area of social service, with impressive results. A willingness on the part of the federal government to respect provincial responsibilities for welfare—and to supply no-strings-attached funding for this purpose—has allowed at least some of the provinces to adopt programs that provide recipients with greater freedom of choice and the opportunity to accept more responsibility for their own well being.

FEDERAL REFORM: RESTORING RESPECT
FOR PROVINCIAL RESPONSIBILITY

In 1996, the federal government replaced the Canada Assistance Plan (CAP) and the Established Programs Finance (EPF) with the new Canada Health and Social Transfer (CHST).[4] Unlike those earlier dollar-for-dollar

---

4 The Canada Health and Social Transfer (CHST) was a combined transfer that provided federal support for provincial health care, post-secondary education, and social assistance and social services programs. On April 1, 2004, the CHST was replaced by the Canada Health Transfer (CHT), which provides federal sup-

cost-sharing initiatives, the CHST provided a block grant to the provinces for spending on welfare, health, and post-secondary education. This block grant reduced total federal funding for those services, transferring more financial responsibility to the provinces. But, critically, it also gave provinces greater authority over how welfare services were to be delivered. The only condition for receiving federal funds for welfare under the CHST (since renamed the Canada Social Transfer—CST) was that provinces must allow residents and non-residents alike to be eligible for social assistance. That is, the federal government prohibited any residency requirement but permitted any other reforms the provinces saw fit. For their part, provinces could use this new flexibility to restructure their social assistance programs.

PROVINCIAL REFORMS: FREEDOM—AND CHOICE

This rebalancing of responsibilities gave Canadian provinces the freedom to experiment. They were able to design programs that best suited the needs of their own people.

Not all chose to pursue reform. Many were satisfied with the basic structure of their welfare programs and did little with the opportunity granted under the new federal legislation. But some provinces set out on a path to reduce dependency and restore hope to their citizens in need. They were able to learn from reforms experienced in other jurisdictions and adjust their policies accordingly. Interestingly however, no two provinces embraced exactly the same set of new policies.

ALBERTA

Alberta began reforming its welfare system even before the CHST, at the risk of losing federal funding. Indeed, the province's success in reducing welfare dependency actually encouraged Ottawa to establish the CHST in

---

port for provincial health-care programs, and the Canada Social Transfer (CST), which provides support for all other programs previously included with health care in the CHST including social assistance and social services.

1996. By the same token, the CHST legitimized Alberta's initiatives and freed the province to pursue them more rigorously.

Most importantly, the Alberta reforms strove to help people avoid welfare in the first place. This approach was based on the recognition that the propensity to receive social assistance increases dramatically after the first receipt of support. Thus, in 1993, Alberta revamped its welfare program with the primary goal of reducing the number of first-time applicants entering the system, particularly young employables.

Case-workers assess the immediate needs of welfare applicants and encourage them to use every other avenue of support, including job-search and labour-market programs, before granting assistance. The goal is to offer more choices and pry open the door of opportunity before dependence sets in with its attendant sense of hopelessness.

Alberta also allowed faith-based non-profit organizations to provide more social services, such as addictions counseling, day care, homeless shelters, and seniors' lodging.

ONTARIO

Ontario also began reform prior to the enactment of the CHST. In 1995, the Ontario government undertook comprehensive measures to reverse a decade-long trend of rising welfare dependency.

Principal among Ontario's reforms was the creation in 1996 of Ontario Works, the first work-for-welfare program in Canada. Its primary goals were to promote self-reliance through employment and provide temporary assistance to those most in need (MCFCS, 2001).

Ontario Works prepares recipients for self-sufficiency by engaging them in some level of employment, depending on their skills, education, and personal or marital status. Though agreements vary, participants typically begin a job search immediately in order to assess their level of employability (MCFCS, 2001). The province instituted private-sector work placements to expand available job opportunities (MCSS, 1999a) while assigning some of those unable to find work through job searches to paid employment in the public sector. Those who criticized Ontario's reduction in welfare benefits—to a level still 10% above the national average—ignored a significant component of this reform. Ontario allowed welfare recipients to keep the same level of total benefits available prior to the benefit reductions by reducing the government share of benefits by 22% and increasing the earnings provisions without "claw-back" by an equal amount. This move further encouraged recipients to start paid work and begin the process of reentering the workforce and learning not only job skills but also life skills associated with having a job (time management, grooming, and so on). To develop work skills among the hardest to employ, typically welfare recipients with little or no work experience, Ontario Works assigned unpaid community service of up to 70 hours per month.

The goal of reform is to open doors of opportunity but sometimes it may also involve a push through that door. In Ontario, recipients who fail to honour their participation agreements are subject to financial penalties. Those who do not adhere to their work requirements, refuse a job without cause, or quit an assigned work placement, have their benefits reduced or cancelled for three months for the first offence, and six months for subsequent offences (Ontario Regulation 134/98). Some have called this hard-hearted but we do a disservice to those who can make better lives for themselves and their families if we allow dependence to grow.

BRITISH COLUMBIA

In 1999, British Columbia for the first time engaged a private-sector agency, JobWave, to assist and support individuals as they rejoined the workforce and regained their independence. In addition to providing a free placement service for employers, JobWave staff provided face-to-face counseling, e-coaching, on-line seminars, and search capabilities for local employment. This innovative re-employment program, one of several operated by WCG International Consultants Ltd., a company based in Victoria, helped over 25,000 British Columbians get back to work between 1999 and 2004.

In 2002, British Columbia became the first province in Canada to experiment with time limits on welfare benefits. Under the new policy, employable recipients were limited to a cumulative two years of social assistance out of every five-year period. Upon the expiration of the time limit, employable recipients become ineligible for welfare while recipients with dependents have their benefits reduced. Effectively, time limits returned welfare to its original purpose: a short-term insurance program to provide assistance in times of emergency. While these time limits were ultimately abandoned, it is interesting to note that their introduction had a signaling effect since their abandonment has not had a large impact on welfare dependency in the province to date.

In addition to the time limits, the province required that all employable welfare recipients, including single parents with children over three years of age, seek employment or participate in job-related activities to remain eligible for assistance. Recipients failing to adhere to their work requirements are sanctioned, resulting in the reduction or cancellation of benefits for a prescribed period. Single parents with children under the age of three were exempt from work requirements. If, after two years, these single parents are not employed, their social assistance benefits were reduced by 33%; only those single parents caring for a disabled child or who are temporarily excused from seeking employment would escape this reduction (Reitsma-Street, 2002).

REFORMS IN OTHER PROVINCES

Not all provinces used their new freedom under the CHST to make comprehensive changes to their welfare systems. Some, such as Saskatchewan and Quebec, implemented far less ambitious reforms. Others maintained essentially the same programs in place before 1996, with only small improvements.

SASKATCHEWAN

Saskatchewan focused on improving incentives to make employment attractive for welfare recipients. In 1997, for example, the Youth Futures program eliminated assistance to individuals younger than 22 years of age unless their families were unable to provide for them financially—while also requiring anyone in this age group who did receive welfare to participate in school, training, or work-experience programs.

QUEBEC

Quebec's changes were even more limited. In 1996, the Quebec government increased the penalty for welfare recipients who failed to look for work or quit a job without legitimate reason. Changes to the treatment of liquid assets sought to ensure that applicants first exhausted all other resources. Adults pursuing vocational high-school education were transferred off welfare to the provincial student assistance plan.

IN SUMMARY

The introduction in 1996 of block grants with minimal constraints freed provinces to experiment with a range of policy alternatives. Some grasped the opportunity to undertake fundamental welfare reforms, adopting focused programs to help people avoid their first stretch on welfare (Alberta), or promptly re-join the workforce (Ontario). Others were content to fine-tune their programs or do very little at all, leaving the basic structure of their welfare systems intact.

THE EVIDENCE: REFORMS PAY HUMAN DIVIDENDS

DEPENDENCY RATES

Between the 1970s and the early 1990s, Canada experienced a considerable increase in welfare dependency in every jurisdiction (figure 5). As we have already noted, by 1994 a record 3.1 million people were receiving social assistance—more than one Canadian in 10. In the wake of reforms, this number has been cut roughly in half. In 2004, just 5.4% of Canadians were receiving assistance.

The fruits of reform have differed by province (figure 6). Alberta experienced a dramatic reduction in the number of people receiving social assistance. In 1993, 196,000 Albertans were on welfare—7.3% of the province's population. That percentage has fallen steadily, to 60,200 people in 2004 (about 1.9% of the population)—a dramatic 69% reduction from the

FIGURE 5: WELFARE DEPENDENCY IN CANADA, 1994 AND 2004

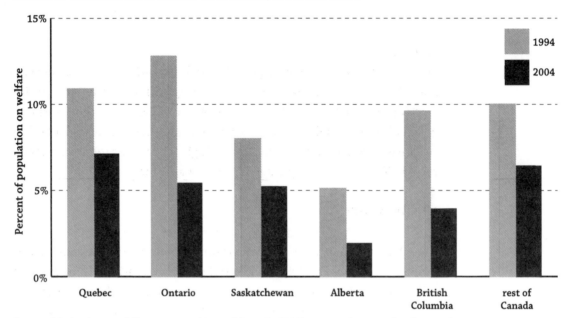

Source: Schafer, Emes, and Clemens, 2001; National Council of Welfare, 2005; Statistics Canada, 2005d.

FIGURE 6: WELFARE DEPENDENCY IN CANADA, 1973–2004

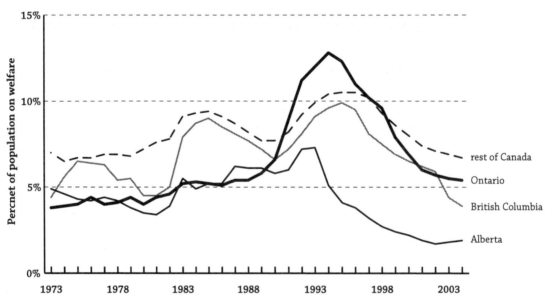

Source: Schafer, Emes, and Clemens, 2001; National Council of Welfare, 2005; Statistics Canada, 2005d.

1993 peak. A similar impact occurred in British Columbia after the 1999 and 2002 reforms. Welfare dependency in that province dropped from 7.5% in 1998 to 3.9% in 2004. Today, British Columbia and Alberta are enjoying the lowest levels of welfare dependency in more than 30 years.

Welfare dependency has also fallen sharply in Ontario. In 1994, 12.8% of Ontarians were receiving welfare cheques. By 2004, that proportion was reduced to 5.4% (or about 672,000 beneficiaries)—the lowest rate of dependency since 1988. Other provinces have had less success in reducing their welfare rolls. Since 1994, Saskatchewan has lowered the number of its dependent citizens from 81,000 (about 8.0% of the population) to 51,800 (5.2%). In Quebec, the rate has fallen from a high of 11.2% in 1996 to 7.1% today; still, aside from Newfoundland (at 9.6%), Quebec has the highest rate of welfare dependency in all of Canada.

In the rest of Canada, where provinces were content mainly to make marginal changes to welfare policies, welfare dependency has declined from an average of 10.0% in 1994 to 6.4% in 2004. This is largely the result of a very strong economy through the late 1990s.

SELF-SUFFICIENCY

Of course, dependency rates do not provide the whole picture. While leaving social assistance is a positive first step, it is also important that former recipients become self-sufficient. To that end, researchers have examined the well-being of welfare leavers in Canada in terms of employment and earnings.

For example, a 2003 survey suggests that British Columbia's reforms have been successful in moving recipients out of dependency and into employment. According to that research, 64% of those leaving welfare found employment, while another 7% returned to school. At the time of the survey, 60% of respondents indicated that their main activity was employment (BC Ministry of Human Resources, 2003).

New data released by Statistics Canada in March 2003 also show that most people leaving welfare have become better off (Frenette and Picot, 2003). The study, *Life after Welfare: The Economic Well-Being of Welfare*

Leavers in Canada During the 1990s, found that about six out of 10 former Canadian welfare recipients saw their after-tax family income improve substantially from what they had received on social assistance. In Ontario, for instance, a third of former recipients earned, on average, $13,000 more than they had received two years earlier on welfare; another third had incomes $2,500 higher than before.

THE POSSIBILITIES: FREEING THE DEPENDENT

PRINCIPLES

It is critical to recognize the central role that our guiding principles of rebalanced federalism, freedom of choice, and acceptance of responsibility have played in the impressive reduction of welfare dependency over the last decade. By the standards of compassion and economy, the results have been heartening and commendable—when those principles have been most vigorously applied.

Provinces that seized the opportunity to make fundamental reforms—especially those emphasizing the choices and responsibilities presented to their citizens in need—have seen their welfare rolls shrink. Most former welfare recipients in those jurisdictions have found employment and become better off. By contrast, provinces that pursued more modest changes have seen relatively smaller reductions in welfare dependency.

However, these principles have yet to be fully or universally applied in social assistance policies. When one level of government provides funding and another designs and delivers programs, accountability and responsibility remained blurred; governments should be fully accountable for the money they raise and spend. Not every jurisdiction has made available to its own needy citizens the same freedom of choice, opportunity, and responsibility for their own lives that are embodied in the 1996 rebalancing of federal roles. We emphasize these points, because these principles guide our recommendations as to "where we go from here."

POLICY PROPOSALS

GETTING THE FUNDAMENTALS RIGHT

While the reforms introduced in 1996 have allowed provinces the freedom to improve their welfare programs dramatically, the current structure of federal transfers is still imperfect. On the one hand, the existing arrangement allows provinces wide latitude to decide policies that lie clearly within their jurisdiction, does not bias their decisions other than to prohibit residency requirements, and allows them to retain surpluses in transferred funds arising from their choices. On the other hand, the transfer still creates a disconnect between the government that raises money for welfare and the government that spends it. Provinces are effectively spending money that they have not collected and thus are likely to be less prudent in the use of those funds. The same disconnect makes governments less accountable to their citizens for how much revenue is really being raised through the taxes they pay.

The federal government would do far better to reduce its revenues by the value of the transfer, vacating the tax room for the provinces to raise their own funds for the purpose of sustaining welfare programs.[5] This gives the provinces a more direct responsibility to their citizens with greater accountability as a result.

Provinces should also take this opportunity to design welfare policies suited to their unique circumstances, policies that best reflect the needs and desires of their citizens. Those provinces that have yet to do so should take advantage of this additional freedom to redesign their welfare schemes to emphasize the "helping hand" over the "warehouse" of long-term dependency.

At the same time, appropriate programs for individuals who do require long-term assistance must reflect the special financial and other needs of these individuals. All too often, disabled Canadians do not receive adequate levels of support to allow them to live in dignity. Even worse,

---

5   A full fiscal examination will be provided in an upcoming volume. Our purpose here is to lay out social programs that work for the people they are intended to help.

"claw-back" measures deprive them of the chance to improve their standard of living by accepting limited employment that is within their abilities.

We have outlined several reforms below that provinces can implement in order to provide a more efficiently administered and delivered welfare program that provides short-term relief to help those in need back to their feet.

IMPROVING THE WELFARE "BACK OFFICE"

Monopolies are nearly always inimical to top performance. An effective welfare program will incorporate competition in both administration and delivery, thereby both reducing costs and improving the quality of services.

1 *Competition in the administration of welfare.*

For-profit companies have certain competitive advantages over the public sector, as do those in the non-profit sector. In order to achieve the most effective administration of welfare services, the system should be open to competitive bidding among both types of organizations.

The United States has permitted the contracting of welfare intake and eligibility determination since 1996. Competition to supply these services has resulted in substantial gains. A leader in this area is Wisconsin, the first state to privatize entire areas of its welfare delivery system through its Wisconsin Works (W-2) program. As a result of opening up eligibility determination, case management, and related services to competitive bidding, the state's taxpayers saved at least $10.25 million during the first two years of privatization (Dodenhoff, 1998). This saving came not through reduced benefits but increased efficiency.

2 *Competition in program delivery.*

As with administrative functions, governments can contract out client-service responsibilities to private for-profit and not-for-profit providers through competitive bidding. As one example, private providers can assist welfare recipients to find and maintain employment through training, trial work periods and post-employment assistance. Such contracts often incorporate a pay-for-performance standard so that providers are compensated based on their success at moving welfare recipients into employment.

One notable example of successful private delivery of welfare is the New York-based America Works. Studies of America Works have found that, of those welfare recipients placed in jobs in the prior three years, 88% were still off the welfare rolls (New York State Department of Labor, 1997). The Social Market Foundation confirmed in its study of America Works that the program had been "successful in helping the long-term unemployed to find jobs and at saving money" (Harding, 1998). Furthermore, the National Center for Policy Analysis found that America Works is capable of training workers for $5,490 per recipient, substantially less than the estimated $24,000 price tag for a comparable program run by New York City (NCPA, 2000).

RESTORING INDEPENDENCE

An effective welfare program both relieves short-term financial distress and assists in the return to economic self-sufficiency. Its objective is one of transition, not maintenance; and its measure of success, you might say, is how quickly it "loses" each client.

1 *Moving forward to employment.*

Opportunity, self-esteem, and future prosperity are all best served by keeping the focus of welfare assistance on the ultimate objective, employment. Programs that concentrate on moving recipients quickly back to work are more effective in generating earnings and self-sufficiency than those that instead emphasize training outside the workplace.

Exposure to the working world helps individuals maintain or acquire basic job skills such as punctuality, reliability, and cooperation. It provides an opportunity to network for future job openings and, perhaps most importantly, earn valuable work experience, the most common barrier to employment for welfare recipients (Reidl and Rector, 2002).

By contrast, empirical evidence largely discredits back-to-work programs that emphasize education and training first. A study by The Fraser Institute of government-sponsored training programs in the United States found that these were largely unsuccessful in reducing unemployment, increasing earnings, or diminishing welfare dependency among poor single parents, disadvantaged adults, and out-of-school youth (Mihlar and Smith, 1997). Similarly, Manpower Demonstration Research Corporation found that recipients placed in employment-focused programs earn 122% more than their counterparts in education-based programs. The same study determined that the employment-first model "moved welfare recipients into jobs more quickly … [and] had larger effects on employment, earnings, and welfare receipt … than [did] education-focused ones" (Hamilton et al., 2001: ES-2).

2 *Making work pay.*

We all need motivation. Incentives are an important policy tool: welfare recipients are more likely to seek and find work when earnings are subject to low effective marginal tax rates. Put another way, when someone can keep most of the income they earn, they are more inclined to work.

All American states offer such incentives in the form of "earned income disregards"—referred to in Canada as "earnings exemptions"— that exclude some income when calculating welfare benefits. Most states also disregard a portion of earnings when determining eligibility (USHHS, 2003). Such exemptions are particularly effective at encouraging part-time employment—valuable in maintaining basic job skills and access to information on future employment opportunities.

Conversely, welfare benefits that exceed what can be earned in the workplace create incentives to remain (or, worse, go) on welfare rather than take employment and be self-sufficient. Thus, benefit levels must be set with regard to prevailing wage rates to ensure that working pays more than welfare.

3 *Making work more than just a goal.*

An explicit requirement that recipients work, with sanctions for those who do not comply, serves both to hasten the transition to self-sufficiency and to make welfare less attractive to first-time applicants. It reinforces the intended temporary nature of social assistance and discourages unnecessary reliance on it.

The United States adopted work requirements with other welfare reforms in 1996. State versions cover a broad range of job-related activities: unsubsidized employment, subsidized private or public-sector employment, on-the-job training, community service, vocational training and job search.

Still, the nature of the required work activity is an important consideration: there are inherent differences between private and public-sector jobs. The latter have often been characterized as temporary "make-work." According to the US General Accounting Office, widespread public-service employment programs of the 1970s failed to prepare participants for unsubsidized work in the private sector (US GAO, 1978, 1979, 1980). Professor Thomas DiLorenzo of George Mason University asserts that the private sector, in contrast, has a greater capacity to develop marketable job skills and foster long-term independence, in part because people are trained in occupations that are valued by employers (DiLorenzo, 1984).

In order to enforce work requirements, every US state has adopted some form of sanctions: welfare benefits are reduced or terminated if recipients fail to participate in their assigned activity.

Evidence from the Wisconsin Works (W-2) program has demonstrated that requiring most new applicants to find employment in the private sector or perform community service shortly after enrolling, reduces the number of entrants by half (Rector, 1997). Similarly the Cato Institute's Michael J. New found that "the strength of state sanctioning policies had the largest impact on caseload declines between 1996 and 2000" (New, 2002: 9).

4 *Setting timelines.*

Limiting the length of time that certain recipients can receive benefits shifts welfare from being a program of entitlement to one of insurance against temporary periods of adversity. It encourages a prompt return to employment and the seeking out of other alternatives to welfare whenever possible. Jurisdictions that have established such time limits have also succeeded in reducing long-term welfare dependency.

Time limits have become the norm in the United States since 1996. Under the federal Personal Responsibility and Work Opportunity Reconciliation Act (PRWORA), American states must impose a five-year lifetime limit on Temporary Assistance for Needy Families benefits. Many have legislated time limits shorter than five years.

The fact that the United States implemented numerous reforms in the late 1990s to reduce welfare dependency makes it difficult to isolate the effect of time limits alone. Nonetheless, certain studies have demonstrated their effectiveness. For instance, a recent study entitled *Welfare Dynamics under Time Limits* examined the effects of Florida's Family Transition Program five-year time limit on the receipt of welfare benefits. The study found that time limits, "in the absence of other features of the program that worked to increase welfare use, would have reduced welfare receipt by as much as 16%" (Grogger and Michalopoulos, 2003).

5 *Creating better options.*

A further strategy helps applicants avoid welfare altogether by pursuing every viable alternative. This is important because one's first spell on social assistance is seldom the last. In other words, receiving social assistance for the first time tends to generate welfare dependency in the future (Blank and Ruggles, 1994; Cao, 1996; Meyer and Cancian, 1996).

In Canada, Alberta has embraced this strategy with the most vigour. In a 1997 study of the province's welfare program, it was determined that "[t]he significant reduction [in the number of recipients] came from a sharp decrease in individuals who were applying for welfare for the first time" (Boessenkool, 1997: 11–12).

WHERE COMPASSION COUNTS MOST: INCREASING HELP FOR THE DISABLED

Welfare works best as a temporary program to help people in need get back on their feet. Regrettably, many disabled Canadians can never be fully self-supporting; they may also face special financial pressures because of their disability. These citizens nonetheless deserve the opportunity to improve their quality of life. The provinces should establish separate programs for these Canadians, providing sufficient support for them to live in dignity. "Claw-backs" and other road-blocks that restrict their ability to supplement these programs with earned income should be eliminated.

WHAT WOULD THESE REFORMS MEAN FOR CANADIANS IN NEED?

If you are on welfare today, these reforms would help you and your family escape the cycle of dependence and poverty. They would give you the assistance, knowledge, experience, and encouragement you need to rejoin the workforce and build a better life.

If you are a single parent, you would no longer be trapped by passive, impersonal assistance that gives you money but little else. Instead, caseworkers would help you find daycare, meet other needs, and search for a job.

The best providers available, chosen through competitive bidding, would put you together with advisors who have a proven track record of understanding your circumstances and helping people like you find opportunity.

When you do find employment, you would keep more of your hard-earned money. You would no longer need to fear losing more in benefits than you gain in wages.

If you fear that welfare may soon be your only recourse, these same competitive, proven social agencies would exert every effort to identify other, better, alternatives.

Instead of representing an indefinite sentence of dispiriting dependency, welfare would at last live up to its name: opening the door to self-confident independence, choice and opportunity, economic freedom, and personal prosperity.

SUMMARY

Our goal can be simply stated: to provide a helping hand to those in need, to help Canadians who encounter hardship regain the dignity of work and the advantages it brings, to restore their hope for a better future. The programs we have discussed are not revolutionary or even new. They have a proven track record in meeting these goals.

Only hesitancy and lack of foresight hold us back. Those are not reasons to abandon hundreds of thousands of our fellow citizens to needless dependency. We owe it to them to move ahead.

In addition, let us never lose sight of the fact that the most important policies to help welfare recipients are not actually welfare policies. Instead, they are policies designed to increase prosperity, jobs, and opportunities. In the first publication of this series, we outlined proven policies to promote growth and reduce unemployment, ideas that we will expand on in future documents. We believe that the reforms to welfare we propose, set beside our broader economic policies, would create new hope and opportunity, particularly for poor Canadians, across the nation.

3 PROVIDING CANADIANS THE WORLD'S BEST HEALTH CARE
HEALTH CARE POLICY IN CANADA

We envision a health care system in Canada that is second to none in the world. We believe Canadians should get the best medical care available—without delay—regardless of ability to pay.

But what is the reality? Canadians pay top dollar for their health care system yet suffer mediocre service and outcomes. Even worse, millions of Canadians endure unnecessary anxiety and deteriorating health as they wait in lengthy queues for diagnosis or treatment to become available.

THE NEED: HELPING CANADIANS ENJOY THE BEST POSSIBLE HEALTH

Canadians deserve the best health care system in the world. We are certainly paying for a world-class system by international comparisons. But Canadians in need of medical services are not getting the results they deserve.

Canadians requiring tests or treatment should receive them promptly. Canada's public health care program should deliver the care Canadians desire in a time frame that gives comfort and peace of mind and—most importantly—supplies treatment when it is most effective, not merely convenient to health bureaucrats.

Every Canadian should receive the highest quality of service, without delay and without regard to income. No Canadian should be forced into an agonizing wait for inferior or insufficient care.

Where government programs fail Canadians' health care needs, they should have the freedom to take responsibility for themselves and arrange for their own diagnostic tests and treatment.

Canadians also deserve choice. They should be able to determine the health-care provider they prefer, whether it be a private for-profit, not-for-profit, or government-administered clinic or hospital. Likewise, Canadians should be able to purchase the health insurance programs that meet their needs.

WHAT IS BEING DONE?
SYMPTOMS OF DISTRESS

The good news is that Canadians are living longer and healthier lives than they were 30 years ago. The bad news is that while Canada ranks third in expenditure on health care as a share of GDP among all the OECD countries with universal-access health systems, we place nowhere near the top in either access to or quality of the health care we actually get (table 1).

According to a recent study of access to health care, Canada ranked twenty-fourth among 27 countries for which data were available in the number of doctors per capita (2.3 doctors for every 1000 Canadians). With respect to advanced medical technology, we ranked thirteenth of 22 in access to MRIs, seventeenth of 21 in access to CT scanners, seventh of 12 in access to mammographs, and were tied for last of 16 nations in our access to lithotriptors.

In 2005, Canadians could expect to wait 17.7 weeks—*more than four months*—after their general practitioner or family doctor said a specialized treatment was necessary before they were actually cared for. That wait was fully 90% *longer* than it would have been only 12 years ago, back in 1993.

Our health is paying the price. Despite spending more on health care than any other industrialized country in the OECD except Iceland and Switzerland, Canadians rank twenty-second in the percentage of our life expectancy that we can expect to live in full health. We rank twentieth in infant mortality, twelfth in prenatal mortality, tenth in deaths due to

TABLE 1: PERFORMANCE OF HEALTH SYSTEMS IN OECD COUNTRIES

	Mortality based on population statistics			Mortality closely related to the effectiveness of health care				
	Healthy life expectancy / life expectancy Rank 2001	Infant mortality Rank 2002	Perinatal mortality Rank 2002	Mortality amenable to health care Rank 2000	Potential years of life lost Rank 2000	Breast cancer mortality Rank 2002	Colon/ rectum cancer combined mortality Rank 2002[1]	Cumulative Rank of disease level indicators
Australia	9	15	9	3	6	5	2	1
Sweden	2	2	8	5	2	1	9	2
Japan	1	3	2	2	3	11	4	3
Canada	**22**	**20**	**12**	**4**	**8**	**10**	**2**	**4**
Iceland	18	1	1	[12][2]	1	4	7	4
Switzerland	6	12	24	[12][2]	4	9	1	6
France	12	7	18	1	12	6	11	7
Luxembourg	2	18	16	[12][2]	7	6	6	8
Italy	9	13	9	9	9	11	5	9
Norway	6	6	15	7	5	8	14	9
Finland	11	3	3	13	10	2	14	11
Korea	27	23	5	[12][2]	21	3	7	12
Germany	5	10	11	12	11	14	12	13
New Zealand	23	24	13	11	16	13	10	14
Spain	4	5	6	6	14	21	18	15
Austria	15	7	13	14	13	16	17	16
Netherlands	12	15	23	8	15	23	16	17
United Kingdom	20	21	18	18	19	15	13	18
Greece	12	22	25	15	17	17	19	19
Belgium	8	14	20	[12][2]	18	18	20	19
Denmark	19	11	17	10	22	21	25	21
Poland	28	26	22	[12][2]	25	20	22	22
Ireland	20	18	27	17	20	24	21	23
Portugal	24	15	6	16	24	19	23	23
Czech Republic	15	9	4	[12][2]	23	25	24	25
Turkey	15	28	[13][2]	[12][2]	[19][2]	28	28	26
Slovak Republic	25	27	20	[12][2]	26	27	26	27
Hungary	25	25	26	[12][2]	27	26	27	28

Note 1: Combined mortality is the average of male and female mortality percentages. Note 2: Not all information was available for all nations. Where data was unavailable, the rank of average values has been inserted in brackets.
Sources: Esmail and Walker, 2005.

breast cancer, eighth in the number of years of life expectancy lost to disease and fourth in avoidable deaths (Esmail and Walker, 2005b).

Canadians believe strongly that health care is vital to their quality of life, and that no Canadian should be denied medically necessary services because of an inability to pay. They may disagree about which policies are most likely to sustain and improve our health care but there is little dispute over the objective itself. Sadly, differences of opinion over which policies work best, combined with fears and illusions about the US health care experience, have locked us into policies that do not serve us well.

Canadians are left wanting, deserving, and paying for more, but getting less and less as time goes on.

DIAGNOSIS: BALANCE DISORDER

Canadian health care suffers from a debilitating disorder: a systemic imbalance of responsibilities and restricted freedom of choice. No other country in the developed world—even those with highly socialistic governments—goes to the lengths that Canada does to insist on a government-planned health care monopoly, regardless of cost.

The keystone of Canada's public health care system, The Canada Health Act (CHA), explicitly denies provinces and individual citizens alike the freedom to seek out policies and services that best suit their own needs. As the current federal government interprets it, the CHA imposes on every province a public-sector monopoly on health care insurance; it dictates that government alone finance and administer all core health care services; and it denies Canadians the right to acquire such services from private providers. The CHA further forbids user charges, extra billing for publicly insured services, or any other market mechanisms and pricing signals that could help allocate health-care resources more efficiently.

Provinces that depart from the Canada Health Act face sanction. They risk losing sizeable federal transfers for health care—estimated at more than $20 billion in 2005/2006.

Do these monopolistic provisions result in better health care? Based on international comparisons, the answer is emphatically "No!" Among OECD countries whose citizens enjoy universal access to health care and also lose fewer years of life to disease and preventable deaths than Canadians, *all* also permit private alternatives to the public system and employ some form of public health care user fee. Furthermore, only two of these countries spend more on health care than Canada, after adjusting for the age of their population (necessary, since the cost of health care varies greatly with age). All of the countries whose populations live more of their life in full health than Canadians, also have a private care sector competing to meet patient needs; over three quarters of these also have some form of cost sharing for access to the system.

When we look at mortality from breast cancer, a specific catastrophic but treatable disease, Canada ranks tenth among OECD nations. Every country with universal-access health care that does better by that measure, also has private health care alternatives and some form of user fees. All but two spend less of their GDP on health care than Canada does.

Finally, few developed countries subject their citizens to such long delays for medical treatment. Seven OECD nations have virtually no waits for care at all; every one has embraced competition, freedom, and personal responsibility throughout its health care programs.

Canada is a rich nation. Our people, including our doctors and other health care professionals, are talented and hard working. When Canadians receive sub-standard care, it is not for lack of wealth or talent. It is a symptom of bad policy. We believe Canada can do better.

LOOKING UP: ENCOURAGING PROSPECTS FOR CHANGE

The preceding sections of this document have recorded how the principles of freedom of choice, personal responsibility, and appropriately balanced federalism have maintained Canada's education system in robust health and begun to restore effectiveness to provincial welfare policies. The poor condition of Canada's public health system is symptomatic of what happens when these same principles are disregarded.

In short, we have been heading down the wrong road: far too great a reliance on a public sector monopoly over the delivery of health care, far too little freedom of choice and acceptance of personal responsibility, and far too much federal interference in an area of provincial jurisdiction. But there are, at long last, encouraging signs that we are being obliged to stop going down that road and seek a new direction.

The recent Supreme Court decision in the *Chaoulli* case sent a powerful warning signal that the delays incurred by our current approach to health care violate Canadians' Charter rights to life and security of the person. It has always been unconscionable for a sick person in Canada to suffer or even die while waiting for public health care. The Court is now telling us—and our governments—that it is also unconstitutional, at least in Quebec.

Significantly, it is Quebec that has been leading the way toward a health care system that continues to assure universal access but allows for a choice of providers. It is moving from a system dominated by government monopoly to a "mixed system."

Recently Alberta has also announced what it calls The Third Way to health-care delivery. Its approach is neither the current Canadian system, with its federally dominated, public sector monopoly, nor the US system, which lacks the universal coverage that Canadians value so highly. Instead, Alberta's "Third Way" will adopt a path taken by two dozen other countries where universal coverage generates better health care outcomes than Canadians experience. It is characterized by universal coverage and access but a "mixed approach" (public and private) to health-care delivery, payment, and insurance.

The medical profession, represented by the Canadian Medical Association, has also indicated a willingness to stop, look around, and consider alternatives to the status quo.

TREATMENT: WHAT MORE CAN BE DONE

PRINCIPLES

Compassion, not money, should be our key concern in reforming Canada's health care system. Our neighbors and fellow citizens in ill health or awaiting test or treatment must be our first priority. But we also believe that the formula for providing them with the prompt, effective, and compassionate care they deserve, lies in the principles we have discussed throughout the *Canada Strong and Free* series.

The Supreme Court's recent decision reflected several of these principles. We Canadians should assume greater personal responsibility for our own health and that of our families. But to do so, we must also have greater freedom to choose the health care services we desire. Federal *fiat* should not limit our choice to a government monopoly. Government agencies need not run hospitals any more than doctors need be civil servants.

Nor should our provincial governments be coerced into denying Canadians alternatives that clearly lie within their constitutional authority. The provinces must be freed from federal shackles to deliver the choices Canadians deserve and demand.

Here once again, the importance of balance between the federal government and the provinces can hardly be overstated. Free of federal constraint, Canada's primary and secondary schools manifest the excellence and diversity that provincial governments, closer and more responsive to their citizens' values and priorities, can mobilize. Likewise, hundreds of thousands of Canadians in need or on social assistance began to gain new hope and opportunity once the federal government recognized that the same could hold true for welfare programs.

The same principle can also lead to new hope and help for Canadians in need of prompt, effective, and appropriate medical attention. At the provincial level, we urge governments to embody the same spirit, by empowering individual Canadians and their families and communities to make their own choices. At the end of the day, health is the most personal of all concerns. Needs and preferences are specific to individuals: they differ materially from family to family, community to community. Governments, even at the provincial level, find it extremely difficult, if not impossible, to aggregate the choices and requirements of millions of individuals and still manage them well. Informed individuals, families, and local communities will always make decisions that reflect their own priorities better than government. Likewise, the health care providers closest to those informed individuals, families, and communities will respond most effectively to their needs and wishes. They must be allowed to do so.

Information and incentive are keys to unlocking this virtuous dynamic. At present, our health care system does little to reward Canadians who exercise responsibility by pursuing healthy lifestyles. Nor does it provide either pricing signals or metrics of quality to guide individuals, families, and communities to sound health care choices.

Nothing better illustrates this perverse aspect of our health care system than its tortured lines of "accountability." Health care providers get most of their revenue directly from governments rather than from the consumers they ostensibly serve. Inevitably, they are more responsive to bureaucratic direction from above than to patient demand from below. The result? Inferior, more expensive, services and unacceptable waits for medically necessary services. When individuals and families have choices in health care—as they do in virtually every other developed nation—they are able to hold health care providers directly accountable. They can demand better—and get it.

Canadians deserve no less. We therefore offer the following policy recommendations for both the federal and provincial governments.

PROPOSALS FOR REFORM

POLICY RECOMMENDATIONS FOR THE FEDERAL GOVERNMENT

1 *Give health care resources back to the provinces.*

This priority is straightforward and compelling: Ottawa should step back from collecting taxes for health care and allow the provinces to raise their own revenues by an amount equivalent to current federal spending for health care delivery.

This can be accomplished if Ottawa reduces the federal personal income-tax rate from 16% to 15% for the lowest bracket, eliminates the next two brackets, and reduces the top federal tax rate from 29% to 25%. These measures would make available to provincial governments tax "room" equal to the current federal spending on health care.

This proposal may alarm Canadians in some lower-income provinces. It need not. A future volume of the *Canada Strong and Free* series will show how a properly structured equalization formula, implemented alongside the reductions in tax rates, can protect them from any negative consequences from this change. In particular, they should note that a reformed equalization formula will provide additional revenues to those lower-income provinces for which a tax "point" is worth less than for higher income provinces.

2 *Spend federal dollars where it makes the most sense.*

Federal support for health care should be directed where it does the most good: on health care science and research; the collection and provision to consumers of information about best medical practices; the portability of benefits between provinces; and the coordination of a national response to health threats that do not respect provincial borders, such as those posed by SARS, BSE, and predicted pandemics.

POLICY RECOMMENDATIONS FOR CANADA'S PROVINCES
Many of the problems plaguing Canadians' health care—waiting lists, lack of the latest medical equipment, shortages of doctors—arise because our system of providing care is organized mainly as a government monopoly. There are much better ways to do things, ways that are entirely consistent with the goal of providing Canadians with prompt and universal access to high quality medical services, regardless of their ability to pay.

The following proposals are made with those goals in mind. Most can be implemented very quickly and would dramatically improve the state of health care in Canada.

1 *Provincial health ministries of the right size.*

The provinces should not respond to the federal government's withdrawal from the health policy sphere by bulking up their own bureaucracies. Rather, provincial ministries should reorganize to fund and regulate—but not deliver—health care services. Governments that both provide and regulate any service face a deep conflict of interest. They should instead conclude and monitor contracts with hospitals, clinics, physicians, and other providers to deliver health services.

Those contracts should establish desired outcomes—such as mortality, infection and complication rates, and patient satisfaction—that provincial authorities should monitor, making the results public to equip citizens to make the best possible choices about where to seek care. Providers who do not live up to the established benchmarks should have their contracts terminated.

On the other hand, contracted hospitals and other service providers should be legally and functionally independent of government. This will free them to conclude their own labour agreements and exercise their own judgment about such questions as how many staff to employ or what sort of equipment to acquire. Facilities that provide publicly funded care should also be accredited by a responsible third party, such as the provincial college of physicians and surgeons or medical association, rather than the provincial government.

2 *Give Canadians the freedom to care for themselves.*

Canadians in every province should be free to contract for private health care services and to buy insurance that would pay for those services.

The present lack of choice in the health care system has resulted in a common, uncontested, and mediocre standard of service, which Canadians are unable to protest by opting for a different provider. Since Canadians cannot "vote with their dollars" by patronizing providers that offer greater convenience, more timely service, better accommodations, or higher quality care, the public health system is not motivated to offer them either. Allowing a parallel, private health sector to flourish will right many of these wrongs. Allowing physicians and hospitals to work under both the privately and publicly funded regimes will serve to import innovations and efficiencies more rapidly from the private sector into the public system.

At present, the provision or purchase of private insurance for "medically necessary" health services is generally disallowed in Canada. When, and if, the Supreme Court's *Chaoulli* decision is implemented, Quebec will be the notable exception to this rule.

This policy ignores the evidence on the pitfalls of having a public monopoly in health insurance. While private health insurance will clearly not solve every health care woe by itself, it will undoubtedly improve the provision of care to all Canadians.

Families, individuals, unions, businesses, volunteer groups, and charities should all be free to buy whatever insurance they wish for themselves or their members. Indeed, they should be encouraged to do so through a program modeled on those in Australia, Germany, and The Netherlands, where purchasers of private health insurance are partly reimbursed, or exempted from paying, the premiums that apply to the public health insurance scheme.

Actively encouraging the development of a private market in health insurance and care delivery could have many benefits, principal among them better service for patients. Patients who buy private health coverage or care with their own money also free up resources in the public system for patients who are waiting to receive them.

3 *Increase accountability.*

Many provinces already report to their citizens how long they will need to wait for certain kinds of care and how many people are ahead of them in the queue. The idea behind these initiatives should be extended to help patients make sound decisions about which hospital or health provider will best meet their needs.

However, while provinces should make more information available to citizens, they should cease being the sole provider of that information. Governmental reviews of government's own performance are inherently suspect. Making it easier for researchers and consumer organizations to access all the data on the health system's activities and performance (while of course protecting individual patients' privacy) would provide a more reliable and richer basis for consumers to determine their best health care choices. The free transparent marketplace for information would encourage providers to compete on the basis of quality.

4 *Work with the private sector.*

International experience indicates that public-private partnerships (P3s) could result in more creatively designed health care facilities, while lowering lifecycle costs by between 20% and 30%. Other reviews are more cautious about P3s; they point to such problems as governments failing to properly enforce contractual arrangements or concluding deals with the private sector without considering competitively priced public ventures. These potential failings on the part of governments should not however obscure the ability of P3s to provide new infrastructure at lower cost and in a more timely fashion than would have been possible without competitive bidding. They deserve consideration.

5 *Pay hospitals for the care they deliver.*

In general, hospitals in Canada today receive an annual operation budget from their provincial health plan. While this system allows provinces to control expenditures, it also disconnects funding from the provision of hospital services. Hospitals have no financial incentive to provide better access or a more comfortable environment to attract more patients. Put simply, hospital administrators see empty operating rooms as savings and suffer no loss if patients decide they will be better cared for at another facility. The result: fewer services and a lower standard of patient care.

Replacing this scheme with payments based on the number and types of conditions actually treated would create powerful incentives to deliver more and better health services without dramatic cost increases. Health economists refer to this method of paying for hospital and surgical care as the "diagnostic related group" (DRG) system, although it is best considered a prospective fee-for-service regime. The idea is fairly simple: the service provider is paid a fee for each individual treated based on the expected costs of treating the patient's diagnosis at the time of admission. Such payments create incentives for hospitals to treat more patients (an idle operating room is no longer saving money but rather wasting it) and to provide the types of services that patients desire. It also sharpens competition among hospitals because the cost of performing procedures is clearly identified.

6 *Encourage patients to make more informed decisions.*

When individuals pay no direct charge for health care at the point of service, they have no financial incentive to restrain their use of health care and limited incentive to make an informed decision about when and where it is most appropriate to seek out care. The situation can produce excessive demand for care and waste resources. Co-insurance, deductibles, and co-payments can increase efficiency in health delivery and reduce costs.

Of course, such mechanisms should be constrained by appropriate limits to ensure that the chronically ill and those suffering catastrophic health events are protected from financial strain. And since cost sharing can have an adverse effect on the health of the poor, these and certain other groups should be exempt from sharing the cost of care altogether.

7 *Free Canada's medical schools to train the doctors Canadians need.*

Much of the current shortage of physician in Canada is the direct result of provincial intervention. Governments chose to down-size medical schools, limit post-graduate enrollments, and resist accrediting international medical graduates. Another part of the problem is the unintended consequence of other decisions, to cap physician billings, close hospitals, and place quotas on some surgeries.

Merely relaxing the existing restrictions on medical school admissions, as now planned, will not resolve the problem in the long term. Instead such restrictions should be abandoned entirely, freeing medical schools themselves to determine their level of admissions. At the same time, permitting medical schools to price their training at its actual cost will allow students themselves to decide whether a career in medicine is profitable, given open supply to the marketplace.

This reform would allow patients' needs—not an arbitrary funding decision—to determine the national supply of doctors. Doctor shortages would be mitigated automatically, as students reasonably anticipate greater returns to their medical education from rising demand (more patients available to attend their practice, patients with unmet health needs, and so on), while excess physician supply would have the opposite effect.

We recognize that changing the system of medical education involves not only health policy but also post-secondary education, income-tax policy, and the medical associations. It is a change not to be taken lightly; as with the other recommendations offered here, it must be thoroughly studied and properly implemented.

8 *Help Canadians save for future medical needs.*

The proportion of Canadians older than age 65 is increasing. While this may or may not foreshadow a future crisis in health care funding, there is no question that seniors consume more health care dollars than non-seniors. It makes sense to prepare for that eventuality by setting aside resources now to guarantee that services are available for tomorrow's elderly without placing undue stress on the coming generation to fund their care.

Quebec's Clair Commission on health care has proposed that that province institute and manage a mandatory collective savings plan to fund future long-term care for its seniors. But rather than yet another massive government program, why not individualized savings accounts for long-term care? As individuals reach an age when they require extra assistance they or their families—not government—could elect whether home support or institutional care best suits their needs. Even easier would be to abandon contribution limits on RRSP and RPP savings plans and allow withdrawals from these existing savings instruments for health purposes. In addition, the interest earned on RRSP and RPP savings, which compounds over time, would substantially increase the resources available to individuals well beyond the actual value of their contributions.

Measures already exist to protect someone's health and financial interests when they lose their autonomy and are unable to manage their assets. These could apply to any savings account.

9 *Empower Canadians to make their own decisions about health insurance.*

Paying for health care through our taxes, as most Canadians do now, begets a number of unfortunate results. With no clear connection between the money being paid into the system and the benefits being paid out, it's possible for governments to increase taxes, claiming the increases are needed to pay for health services, without dedicating the additional revenues that result to that end. As well, when citizens do not share the cost of the health services they receive at the point of access, they may resist tax increases that truly are required—failing to make (or doubting) the connection with the health care they demand as though it were free. This can lead to chronic shortfalls in health care funding.

A better solution, common in Europe, is what is known as "social insurance"—essentially, a system of either private or public insurers (or both) at arms-length from government that provide coverage for health care costs. To ensure universal access to care, enrolment is mandatory: every citizen would have to choose, and pay premiums to, one of a number of competing social insurance providers. Some tax financing may still be required to provide coverage for the poor, the unemployed, and possibly the elderly. Still, this system is less vulnerable to politically motivated intervention than a fully tax-financed system, as independent bodies collect the insurance payments and dispense the funds for health services.

In the Czech Republic, Germany, and Switzerland, social insurers compete for customers, sometimes offering a variety of cost-sharing schemes that allow those willing to pay more out of pocket to enjoy lower premiums. At the same time, the presence of multiple purchasers of health services encourages competitive efficiencies among providers.

There may be other benefits: countries that have opted for a social insurance system of health funding have fewer problems providing prompt care than those that have a tax-financed system (Altenstetter and Björkman, 1997). A comparison of Britain's publicly funded National Health Service with California's private, non-profit Kaiser Permanente, meanwhile, found that the per-capita costs of the two systems were similar to within 10%. Yet Kaiser members experienced more comprehensive and convenient primary care as well as quicker access to specialists and hospital admissions (Feachem, Sekhri, and White, 2002).

WHAT WOULD THESE REFORMS MEAN
TO YOU AND YOUR FAMILY?

If these reforms were adopted, how would your experience of health care change? Most importantly, you and your family would continue to be fully insured against catastrophic illness, just as you are now. Your access to all medically necessary services would continue to be assured, regardless of your ability to pay. Indeed, that access would be enhanced: no longer would you need to fear being placed on a waiting list for tests or treatment for months on end, experiencing anxiety while your health possibly was placed at risk.

In most provinces, when you are sick you would still most likely enter the health care system through the door of a doctor's office, clinic, or hospital, with your bill paid by the public health-insurance program. But if your needs could not be attended to promptly or satisfactorily there, you would have other options. You might ask to be referred to another facility offering equivalent or more specialized care where you could be treated sooner. That facility, however, might well be financed and operated by a qualified private operator.

If the services provided by the private facility were core services covered by your provincial health care insurance plan, you might choose to present your Health Care Card and have some of the cost of your treatment covered by that plan in accordance with the same fee schedule used at publicly run facilities, while you pay a little extra on top. On the other hand, if the services you require or desire are not covered by your provincial health care plan, you may choose, or be required, to pay for the entire service yourself, either from your pocketbook or using your private health insurance (which is the case now).

In addition to more choice in services, you may also be presented with obligations and incentives to assume more personal responsibility for your own health. This will likely take the form of more "cost sharing" between you and the province for some of your health care, through a combination of user fees, insurance premiums, deductibles, and co-payments. Encountering these payments will certainly make you more aware of what health service alternatives cost; it may also make you more discriminating in your health care choices.

You may also find that your federal tax bill is lower but that you are paying an amount close to the reduction in premiums to a public or private social insurance fund. At the same time, your new insurer will allow you to pocket the rewards for looking after your health better than your neighbours in the form of lower premiums.

As your freedom of choice and acceptance of responsibility increase, we believe that you and your family will benefit significantly from increased control over your own health and well-being, more timely services, and lower overall costs for better health care than you now receive.

IN SUMMARY

Our choices are not simply between Canada's government monopoly on the funding and management of health care and the patchwork of private and public insurance and services that leaves too many of our American neighbours without affordable medical treatment. Many health care systems around the world—in Sweden, Japan, Australia, France, Switzerland, and other nations—allow more freedom of choice and individual responsibility than Canadians enjoy, while at the same time guaranteeing everyone, regardless of income, access to high levels of care.

We advocate following their lead and the guiding principles that have already performed so well for us in the areas of education and welfare policy. We propose freeing the provinces and the private sector from stagnant, monolithic, monopoly thinking to innovate solutions to the current health care crisis and meet our future health care needs. National health care standards can be preserved by interprovincial agreement through the new Council of the Federation, while federal equalization payments continue to assist have-not provinces to meet those standards.

Our goal is to provide Canadians with the best health care system in the world, one that will be a true example for others. Our nation possesses the resources, the talents, and the blueprints to accomplish those ambitions. We believe Canadians deserve no less.

4 SUPPORTING PARENTS AND CHILDREN

CHILD CARE POLICY IN CANADA

We envision a Canada that is the best place in the world for children to grow up—where every child experiences the love, care, and opportunity essential to their development. We envision a Canada where every parent has the freedom to bring up their children as they consider best—as well as child care choices that suit their unique needs. In short: a Canada where both parents and government policy "put children first."

But what is the reality? Governments increasingly coerce parental choice, subsidizing some child care options and not others. Thousands of Canadian children are being funneled into formalized daycare, though this is far from their preferred option. Our government continues to divert resources to some of Canada's most prosperous families—those with two wage earners—away from single earner families that often struggle financially to raise their children. This is particularly unfair to poorer Canadians, without the means to make other choices.

THE NEED: HELPING PARENTS BE PARENTS

Childhood is a special time of life. It is when we form the attachments, habits, attitudes, personalities, and fundamental personal skills that will carry us through the rest of our lives. It is not too much to suggest that almost everything truly vital to our success or failure as adults we learn as children.

Canadian children deserve the best possible foundation for later success: an environment that provides the full measure of all these emotional, social, intellectual, and spiritual necessities. Families, not governments, are in the best position to determine what environment will best ensure that their children flourish into happy, secure, and productive adults.

Canadian parents deserve the freedom to make their own decisions about what is best for their children. Every family, particularly those with fewest resources, should be able to count on the help they need to put those choices into effect. None should fear the state's interfering hand in how their children are best raised.

Canadian families deserve to have available to them the option that best fits their children's needs. This includes parenting at home or with a relative; it includes informal daycare, including services run by friends and relatives. And it includes formal daycare.

But Canadian children should never be trapped in a one-size-fits-all system, determined and sanctioned by government policy. Each child is unique; one size will never fit all.

WHAT IS BEING DONE?
BUILDING THE NANNY STATE

The past decade has witnessed a surge of government activism in the area of child care policy—culminating in the five-year, $5 billion initiative the federal government announced in its February 2005 budget. This activism has been justified by social and economic trends that show women joining the work force in record numbers and a growing number of families headed by single mothers.

In 1999, 69% of women with children under 16 were in the paid workforce, up dramatically from 39% in 1976 (Stafford, 2002). Over roughly the same period, the percentage of families headed by single parents (the vast majority of them women) grew from 9.4% in 1971 to 16% in 2004 (Statistics Canada, 2005a). Child care has assumed additional significance in light of provincial reforms intended to encourage welfare recipients, including single parents, to make the transition from dependency to employment (Schafer et al., 2001; Gabel, Clemens, and LeRoy, 2004).

WHO'S MINDING BABY? PATTERNS OF CHILD CARE USE

More families where both parents work and more working single parents, have inevitably meant that more Canadian children are being entrusted to someone other than their parents.

In 2000/2001 (the most recent year for which data are available), 53% of children between the ages of six months and five years received care from someone other than a parent or guardian, up from 42% in 1994/1995 (Statistics Canada, 2005b). The vast majority (75%) of these children are cared for outside of formal daycare. About half (51%) are cared for in someone else's home by a relative or non-relative; about one-quarter (24%) are cared for in their own home by a family member or someone else.

The most significant recent change has been an increased reliance on care by relatives—up 41% between 1994/1995 and 2000/2001 to nearly one child in three (31.5% of all children). Parents across Canada were also more likely to have a relative raise their child at home in 2000/2001 than in 1994/1995. National daycare use also increased during this time period, by 26%. On the other hand, care by non-family members outside a formal daycare fell by 25%.

While reliance on daycare appears to be growing nationally, it is important to note striking differences among provinces (table 2). Daycare is used least in Saskatchewan (10.2% of children) and most heavily in Quebec (41.4%), where daycare is universally available to all parents at the nominal cost of $7 a day (Statistics Canada, 2005b). This policy in Quebec, which priced daycare significantly below other child care choices, contributed to a 64% increase in reliance on daycare there between 1994/1995 and 2000/2001, and a concomitant drop in care by relatives (to barely 2% of all children) and other home-based care (28%). Because Quebec represents approximately one-quarter of Canada's population, this massive shift produces a statistical overstatement of the growth in formal daycare use nationally.

Not every province saw a growing number of parents rely on formal daycare during the study period. In Alberta, Saskatchewan, Ontario, and Newfoundland, daycare use fell. At the same time, it increased substantially

TABLE 2: PATTERNS OF CHILD CARE[1]

	Someone else's home by a non-relative (%)		Someone else's home by a relative (%)		Child's home by a non-relative (%)	
	1994/ 1995	2000/ 2001	1994/ 1995	2000/ 2001	1994/ 1995	2000/ 2001
Canada	43.6	33.9	14.2	17.1	14.2	9.5
Newfoundland and Labrador	19.5	16.2	20.7	22.4	25.0	18.7
Prince Edward Island	40.8	35.1	18.3	15.7	13.9	8.0
Nova Scotia	31.0	26.3	12.6	22.6	25.5	13.3
New Brunswick	40.4	34.6	17.2	18.7	14.8	12.6
Quebec	42.7	33.6	15.1	11.3	13.1	6.4
Ontario	44.2	35.8	12.4	18.4	13.2	10.1
Manitoba	51.4	37.6	17.8	18.8	10.8	7.7
Saskatchewan	57.4	53.5	15.7	15.6	10.5	9.9
Alberta	46.0	32.7	12.0	19.2	12.3	9.5
British Columbia	40.2	25.4	17.7	22.2	20.9	12.2

Note 1: Table 2 shows main child-care arrangement for children six months to five years of age.
Sources: Statistics Canada, 2005b; calculations by authors.

in British Columbia, Manitoba, and New Brunswick, in the absence of universal or low-cost daycare programs in those provinces.

These provincial variations highlight the importance of giving provinces the freedom to set policies that reflect the unique needs and preferences of their citizens.

ARE WE HEADING IN THE WRONG DIRECTION?

The Vanier Institute recently surveyed Canadians, asking them to rank seven child-care choices by their preference, on a scale of one to five. On average, parents picked day care dead last. That was not surprising, considering that the study also found that 90% of mothers and 84% of fathers who were working full-time would prefer to work-part time and care for their child at home if they could afford it (Bibby, 2004).

Interestingly, public opinion on this issue crosses party lines. In a 2003 Compas survey of Ontario voters, 67% of confirmed Conservative

Child's home by a relative (%)		Daycare centre (%)		Change in daycare use (%), 1994/2005–2000/2001	Change in care at home by a relative (%), 1994/2005–2000/2002
1994/ 1995	2000/ 2001	1994/ 1995	2000/ 2001		
8.1	14.4	19.9	25.0	26%	78%
19.1	28.9	15.8	13.8	–13%	51%
9.3	13.1	17.7	28.1	59%	41%
11.0	16.7	20.0	21.2	6%	52%
7.3	12.3	20.2	21.8	8%	68%
3.9	7.3	25.2	41.4	64%	87%
11.2	16.9	19.0	18.8	–1%	51%
6.4	13.7	13.6	22.3	64%	114%
4.4	10.8	12.1	10.2	–16%	145%
6.1	16.5	23.6	22.0	–7%	170%
8.4	19.7	12.9	20.5	59%	135%

voters, 58% of Liberals, and 64% of NDP supporters preferred care by a relative as a second choice to a parent staying home to care for an infant or pre-school child (Compas, 2003). These polling data suggest that, absent policies that bias parents towards one specific form of care (as in the case of Quebec), actual patterns of child care in Canada roughly reflect parental preferences.

Nevertheless, the federal government has promised to spend billions on a new national system that favours formal, institutional care over other private and family-based alternatives. This federal initiative threatens to lead us onto the same road—since abandoned—that we once went down with respect to social assistance: heavy-handed, monolithic, federal interventions that too often felt to recipients more like a trap than a helping hand. Moreover, it ignores the principles of freedom of choice, personal responsibility, and balanced federalism that, as we have seen, underlie Canada's achievements in education and are so desperately needed as remedies to our ailing health care system.

Surely to organize two different but related services for children—child care and K-12 education—on contradictory principles heading in opposite directions is a formula for disaster. Yet, federal politicians are already comparing the daycare initiative to the development of Medicare. This is cause for alarm: Canadian parents do not deserve this failed model of policy-making.

This is not to say there is no role for government in supporting formal child care settings. Considered as a part of programs designed to get people off social assistance and into the workforce, for example, and weighed against the human and financial cost of long-term welfare dependency, there is a legitimate case for providing limited child care support to low-income single parents.

This underscores the importance of evaluating existing and proposed child care policies in light of other programs intended to support families with children.

In 2004/2005, federal assistance for families with children (including transfers to provinces) amounted to $14.5 billion (table 3). With the new child care program set to increase this figure by more than a third over the next five years, it is critical that we evaluate the effectiveness of this level of spending.

TABLE 3: SPENDING ON FAMILIES WITH CHILDREN ($ MILLIONS)

Maternity Leave (2005)[1]	980
Parental Leave (2005)[1]	2,117
Child Care Expense Deduction (2005)[2]	550
Dependent Deduction (2005)[1]	680
Canada Social Transfers (CST) (2004/05)[1]	650
Early Learning and Child Care Initiative (2004/05)	200
Canada Child Tax Benefit (CCTB) (2005)[1]	9,295
TOTAL	**14,472**

Note 1: Projection. Note 2: This table includes only the portion of the CST directed to child-care initiatives. See Figure 1 for details.
Sources: Government of Canada, 2004, 2005b; HRSDC, 2004b.

DOES FORMAL, INSTITUTIONAL DAYCARE PROVIDE A BETTER CHILDHOOD?

One of the most frequently heard arguments for a universal system of formal, regulated, child care is that it guarantees better outcomes than the more informal care of a parent, relative, or live-in nanny. This argument is contradicted by a growing body of research.

Nationally representative, long-term studies in Canada and the United States suggest that while formal day care and early learning programs can have an initial positive benefit on some children—especially those from low-income and otherwise disadvantaged families—these benefits tend to "fade out" over time (Lefebvre and Merigan, 2002; Gagné, 2003; Magnuson et al., 2004). This is consistent with studies of the US Head Start and the Perry Preschool Project; these also saw initial positive effects, again concentrated among disadvantaged children, "fade out" as they grew older (McKey, 1985; Currie and Thomas, 1997; GAO, 1997). Similarly, Canadian fourth-graders out-score their European counterparts in international reading tests, despite the fact that far fewer young Canadians have spent their early childhood in the supposedly advantageous setting of formal child care.

The absence of long-term cognitive or developmental benefits from formal, regulated child care programs must be set against an extensive body of research associating time spent in day care with increased aggression and other behavioural problems, especially among younger children and infants (see for example NICHD, 2003; Magnuson et al., 2004). These troubling behaviours reflect the importance of infant-mother attachment to a child's healthy development (Belsky and Casiday, 1994; Rutter, 1995; NICHD, 1996; Burchinal, 1999). Other health concerns associated with day care include a higher risk for SIDS (Sudden Infant Death Syndrome) and infections (Rhoads, 2004; Moon, 2000; Ferson, 1994). More frequent infections lead in turn to an overuse of antibiotics, which can make children vulnerable to new and more dangerous forms of disease.

A review of the research makes one fact abundantly clear: the relative benefits of child care alternatives depend primarily on the different personal circumstances (income, education, parenting skills) of families as well as the individual needs of children. Accordingly, the "public benefit" argument does not justify policies that remove responsibility for child care from those who know children best—their parents.

GROWTH SPURT: THE FEDERAL SPENDING RECORD

CONDITIONAL GRANTS

The federal government has been using its spending power to finance a growing array of child care services since 2000, when it signed an Early Childhood Development (ECD) agreement with provinces. That agreement added $2.2 billion over five years to CHST transfers, which provinces were obliged to invest in new ECD programs. An additional $900 million (over five years) was earmarked for early learning and child care in 2003. In February, the federal government bumped these conditional grants up once again, with its promise to fund a universal child care system. Altogether, this adds up to nearly $10 billion in new support for child care over the next five years (figure 7).

While the federal government had hoped to negotiate a single national agreement to attach conditions to this new funding, it failed to

FIGURE 7: CONDITIONAL CHILD-CARE GRANTS, 2004/2005–2009/2010

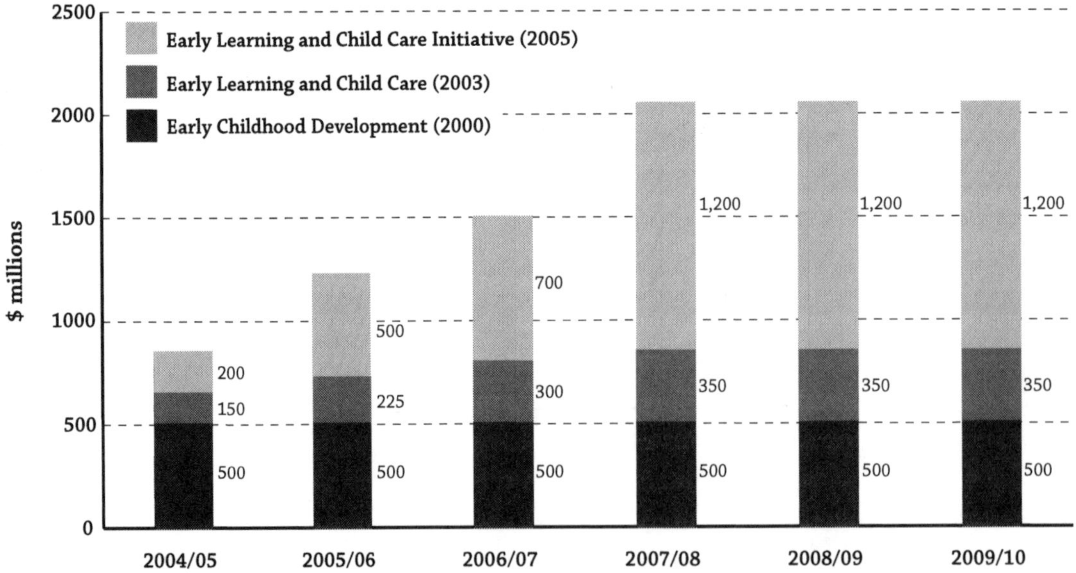

Source: Government of Canada, 2005b: 72, 120.

secure the necessary unanimous provincial endorsement. Undeterred, Ottawa has so far reached bilateral deals with six of the ten provinces, bringing a national child care system closer to reality. As Prime Minster Paul Martin predicted after signing the first bilateral agreement with Manitoba in April, "Decades ago, it was a series of such agreements that led to the creation of Medicare in Canada—a program that now helps to define us as Canadians" (Government of Manitoba, 2005a).

While all these "agreements in principle" require that the new federal funding go toward regulated early learning and child care programs, the provinces retain some freedom in how they deliver those programs. Manitoba, for instance, agreed to subsidize only regulated, non-profit child care providers but has made its first priority raising the wages and training levels of child care workers (Government of Manitoba, 2005b).

Ontario is taking a different approach. Based on European models, Ontario's Best Start program will expand in coming years to provide institutional child care during non-school hours for all four- and five-year-olds enrolled in junior and senior kindergarten—to be extended eventually to all children older than 30 months.

Alberta has signaled a more flexible strategy, allowing for-profit as well as non-profit providers to be eligible for subsidies. Uniquely among the provinces, Alberta also provides a Kin Childcare program, which funds parents to pay a non-resident blood relative to care for their children.

While Ottawa's conditional grants do afford some flexibility, they also threaten to distort provincial priorities that might better reflect their citizens' preferences. Requiring that federal funds be spent only on non-parental child care, for example, disadvantages families that choose to sacrifice income by having one parent stay home to take care of their children. Provinces that accept the federal grants also become obligated to oversee services that families, neighbours, and the many charities and churches of the non-profit voluntary sector previously provided privately and informally. As well, by forcing provinces to direct limited resources into formal child care, conditional grants constrain other options, such as tax cuts, that could make other choices more affordable for Canadian families.

At heart, the "strings attached" funding formula once again gives the federal government leverage to dictate policy priorities in an area of exclusive provincial jurisdiction. This is the same discredited pattern of intervention that has led Canadian health care into a quagmire of mediocrity and the exact opposite of the balanced federalism that has lifted Canadian education to international excellence.

TAX DEDUCTIONS

The federal government also allows working parents to deduct from their annual federal income tax bill up to $7,000 of child care expenses for children under the age of seven, and $4,000 for children between the ages of seven and 16. This Child Care Expense Deduction (CCED) covers formal daycare, day camps, and boarding school—but not care by a parent. This preferential tax break cost the federal government $550 million in 2004/2005 and was directed to non-parental care arrangements, while discriminating against families who choose to care for their children at home.

That bias is not the only one Canadian families must endure. Canada's progressive income-tax system is also biased against families who prefer to have one parent care for the child at home: as table 4 illustrates, a family with a single income equal to the total income of a dual-earner family will face a higher tax bill, because the single earner's income is taxed at a higher marginal rate.

Seventy-one percent of respondents to a 2002 Strategic Council survey either "strongly agreed" (40%) or "somewhat agreed" (31%) that "the current tax system makes it more difficult for families to choose to have one parent stay at home with younger children" (Strategic Council, 2002). This view crossed all party lines, although supporters of what was then the Canadian Alliance were somewhat more likely (78%) than Liberal supporters (68%) to agree that the tax system impeded parental choice.

MATERNITY/PATERNITY LEAVE BENEFITS

Government support for child care also includes increasingly generous parental leave benefits funded by Employment Insurance (EI). First included in the Employment Insurance system in 1971, maternity leave benefits

TABLE 4: CANADA'S INCOME TAX BIAS

	SCENARIO 1			SCENARIO 2		
	Mom	Dad	TOTAL	Mom	Dad	TOTAL
Income	$40,000	$40,000	$80,000	$80,000		$80,000
personal exemption	$7,756	$7,756		$7,756		
spousal exemption				$6,586		
child care deduction		$11,000				
Taxable income	$32,244	$21,244		$65,658		
@ 16%	$24,427	$21,244		$17,841		
@ 22%	$7,817			$32,185		
@ 26%				$15,632		
Total tax paid	$5,628	$3,399	$9,027	$14,000		$14,000
Tax Bias						$4,973

Sources: Veldhuis and Clemens, 2004.

were extended to adoptive parents in 1984; parental leave benefits for either parent were added to those previously reserved for mothers in 1989. In the intervening years, both eligibility for, and the duration of, benefits have been extended. Eligible new parents now receive a combined total of 50 weeks of leave at 55% of their insured income (up to a maximum annual gross income of $39,000). In 2005, these benefits were worth an estimated $3.1 billion—an increase of 169% since 1998 (not adjusting for inflation).

These growing costs are directly related to relaxed eligibility requirements and extended benefits. In 2004, nearly two-thirds (65.9%) of all mothers received parental leave benefits at some point during their pregnancy or after the birth of their child, up from 54.9% in 2000. Over the same period, the length of the average leave increased from seven to 11 months (Statistics Canada, 2005c).

Most new parents surely welcome assistance that reduces the cost of staying at home in the crucial first months of a child's life. Indeed, a 1998 Compas survey found that 89% of parents would prefer to care for their children at home beyond the subsidized leave period if they could afford to (Compas, 1998). A 2002 Strategic Council survey similarly found that three-quarters (76%) of respondents would rather have one parent stay home with their children than place them in some other form of care, if money were not a consideration.

Unfortunately, there is one significant problem with the current parental leave program provided through EI: its sharply unequal treatment of self-employed families that falls especially heavily on women in the workforce.[6] While self-employment has grown rapidly over the past 25 years, especially amongst women, the self-employed (with the exception of fishers, hairdressers, and taxi and other drivers) do not contribute to the EI system. Nor do they qualify for parental leave benefits. As a consequence, nearly one in three self-employed women is back at work three months after giving birth, compared to just 3% of paid workers (Statistics Canada, 2004).

WHAT MORE CAN BE DONE?
LIVING UP TO OUR POTENTIAL

PRINCIPLES

While there are legitimate reasons to include child care help in the overall mix of social programs, many publicly funded child care benefits violate the principles of balanced federalism, parental choice, and, by limiting parental options, the freedom of Canadian families.

The lessons we have stood by in education, are at last learning in welfare, and are still paying for not yet learning in health care, must be heeded in child care: provincial governments are closer to the people they serve than Ottawa and thus in a better position to develop social programs. Once again, Ottawa wants to use its fiscal clout to force choices on provincial policy and thereby onto parents. In addition to distorting prior-

---

6   A more complete treatment of the EI program and sensible policies for reform will be discussed in an upcoming volume of the *Canada Strong and Free* series.

ities, this blurs accountability as the roles of the two levels of government become hopelessly confused. Ottawa must respect the constitutional role of the provinces in managing child care policy.

If provincial jurisdiction is respected, diversity and excellence will flourish in our care of Canada's children outside of school hours just as it has inside the classroom. Canadians can learn from what has proven successful in other parts of the country, avoid what has failed, and develop new initiatives that best reflect their own priorities.

Help for parents should discriminate against none. Assistance should not benefit the rich at the expense of the poor or struggling, as government-funded daycare programs all too often do by favouring two-income families over those that sacrifice to allow one parent to stay at home.

Most importantly, our vision for child care is centered on the family. *Families*, not state bureaucrats or politicians, should make the choices that best suit their needs. This key principle has two sides: families should have the freedom, means, and responsibility for raising children—and government should not interfere in these choices, except in truly exceptional circumstances.

Perhaps most damning of all, most parents put government-supported child care last on their list of preferred choices. According to an Ekos poll conducted in the summer of 2004, just 30% of Canadians favoured more and better child care programs. Nearly twice that number favoured parent-centered assistance: either direct financial subsidies (28% of respondents), tax breaks (21%) or simply information to help parents meet their own needs (18%) (*Windsor Star*, 2005: A9). Similarly, when Ontarians were asked in 2003 to choose whether they would rather have government give money to day cares to reduce costs or give money to parents so they can better afford whatever care they think is best, only slightly more than one in three (35%) indicated that money should be allocated to day care (Compas, 2003). In other historical analyses of preference, Canadian women agreed most frequently and strongly on policies that supported choice in how they care for children (Michalski, 1999).

POLICY PROPOSALS

The following recommendations reflect the preferences that Canadians have repeatedly expressed—but federal leaders have consistently disregarded.

1 *Stop penalizing child care choices with biased tax breaks.*

Government policy should not privilege formal, paid day care over care by a parent or another family member. Families should have the freedom to choose the child care arrangement that is right for them without being penalized through the tax code. To that end, a Universal Child Expense Deduction (UCED) should replace the Child Care Expense Deduction that now covers only the cost of formal, institutional care.

Sixty-five percent of Canadians surveyed by Compas in 1998 felt that "changing the tax law to make it easier for parents with young children to afford to have one parent at home," should be a high or very high priority (Compas, 1998). Accordingly, the current Child Care Expense Deduction should be phased out over a five-year period. Over the same time, the Dependent Deduction currently provided to all tax paying families with children should be gradually increased. While this change will have a neutral effect on federal revenue, the bias towards non-parental child care would be eliminated.

Under this new system, families would face the same tax burden and receive the same amount of federal support (in terms of tax-exempt income) regardless of whether they choose to have their children cared for by an unpaid caregiver within the home or in a formal daycare environment. This universal deduction will give parents greater freedom and personal resources to care for their children in the way that best suits their needs, values, and family circumstances.

2 *Restore federal-provincial balance by eliminating conditional grants.*

Canada is a large and diverse country, a diversity reflected in the different choices that parents in different provinces make for the care of their children. A Canada that believes in strong and free families must respect these differences. As we have seen repeatedly, the government that is clos-est to the citizens it serves is most likely to make the best choices on their behalf. Accordingly, the federal government should abandon its latest attempt to dictate social policy choices through conditional transfers and instead vacate tax room to provinces to pursue their own priorities. This respect for the proper balance of Confederation will have the additional benefit of promoting more responsive, accountable programs.

In the same spirit, provinces fashioning their own distinctive child care policies should adopt a "bottom-up" or demand-driven approach, di-recting subsidies to parents, not selected care providers. This can be done either through a system of tax credits, deductions, or child care vouchers. Bottom-up solutions put decision-making power in the hands of consum-ers and are vastly more efficient.

3 *Support self-employed parents as well as the employed.*

Canadian parents clearly value the opportunity to remain at home in the crucial weeks and months before and after a child's birth. Parental leave programs can assist them by reducing the cost of leaving the labour force temporarily to care for their children. Yet the existing, EI-based, federal leave benefits program clearly fails our growing number of self-employed parents. They deserve better. Legislation should be enacted to allow these parents to fund their own parental leave by accessing their RRSP savings, in the same way that individuals can borrow these funds for home pur-chases or life-long education.

A recent survey by the University of Guelph's Centre for Families, Work and Well-Being found that, while most self-employed women (82% of professionals and 96% of those in lower-earning fields) want access to maternity leave benefits, they would prefer a voluntary scheme to a mandatory, EI-type program (Rooney et al., 2003: 36). Interestingly, this preference persisted even if a voluntary model was more expensive than a mandatory scheme. Put another way, Quebec's mandatory new program for self-employed workers is neither what most self-employed Canadians want nor the most cost-effective option.

Instead, the federal government should allow self-employed individuals to fund their own parental leave by borrowing from their own tax-sheltered retirement savings. Funds withdrawn to support parental leave should be exempt from income tax as long as they were repaid over a period of 10 to 15 years. This voluntary Parental Savings Plan (PSP) would be modeled after the existing First Time Home Buyers Plan, which allows individuals to borrow up to $20,000 from their RRSP towards the purchase of their first home and Life-Long Learning Plans that permit similar borrowing to pay for post-secondary education.

WHAT WOULD THESE REFORMS MEAN TO YOU AND YOUR FAMILY?

As a parent, not only would you have a wider array of choices to care for your children but those options would no longer be constrained by your marital or employment status.

Government programs would no longer push you to enroll your daughter or son in formal, institutional day care over other choices you may prefer. If you are self-employed when your new baby arrives, you would have the option to enjoy much the same parental leave as your employed neighbours. If you prefer to remain at home to care for your child while your spouse continues to go to work, you would no longer be penalized at tax time. All families would receive an equivalent level of help.

Regardless of your circumstances, you would enjoy an expanded choice of child care alternatives. If you work a regular 9-5 job, you would have additional means to pay for centre-based day care. If instead you are a single parent working part-time or work non-standard hours, you would have new resources to pay a relative, neighbour, or nanny to care for your child—in your own home or that of someone else.

Perhaps most importantly, you would be in the driver's seat when it comes to your child's care. You would no longer have to settle for an inflexible, "one-size-fits-all" institutional form of child care. Instead, your autonomy and responsibility to make the choices for your child that best reflect your values would receive the respect—and support—they deserve.

SUMMARY

Our child care objectives for Canada respect parental preferences and reaffirm the pre-eminent role of the family in providing and caring for children. Our recommendations would also reduce unnecessary inefficiencies that drive up the costs of child care. By putting more resources and decision-making power in the hands of parents, the policies we propose will respond to the unique needs and values of every Canadian family.

By trusting parents, rather than a distant government, with the responsibility for their children's care, growth, and early development, these policies reflect the principles of a strong and free Canada.

5 THE ROAD AHEAD

The preceding chapters have described how Canada is moving toward a "rebalancing" of federal and provincial responsibilities in the provision of essential social services. This rebalancing is based on the principles that services to people—especially the young, the ill, and those trapped in poverty—should be delivered by governments and organizations closest to those they serve and should involve a better mix of public and private resources. This rebalancing is most pronounced and has been most successful in the area of K-12 education and welfare. Its application is as yet only being considered in relation to health care; and, with respect to child care, the federal government is still (for some inexplicable reason) moving in the opposite direction.

At the same time, we have seen that where the provinces have been accorded their rightful responsibilities in these areas and have acquired the financial resources to discharge them, there has often been a beneficial "democratization" of social service decision making and delivery—many provinces affording their citizens greater freedom of choice with respect to such services, accompanied by increased personal responsibility.

As stated in *A Canada Strong and Free*, the first volume of this series, we believe that these fundamental principles of re-federalized federalism and democratization are essential, not only to the improvement of social services and quality of life but also to making Canada the best-governed democratic federation in the world. In the third volume of this series, we will focus on the broader application of these principles to the practice of democracy and federalism itself.

We also want to emphasize that at the end of the day the elimination of most of the need for welfare and the generation of the dollars required to adequately fund child care, health care, and educational services, will depend on our success in improving Canada's economic productivity and performance. Improving Canadian productivity and economic performance will therefore be the sole focus of the fourth volume of this series.

The implementation of policies designed to give us the highest quality of life, the best economic performance, and the best in democratic governance and the practice of federalism will raise Canada's international standing to that of a model international citizen and leader. Attaining this status and exerting such international influence will be the primary subject of the fifth volume.

We conclude by renewing our invitation for you to join with us in developing and refining the public policies presented in this and future volumes—policies to bring into being a future Canada that is truly strong and free.

REFERENCES

Altenstetter, Christa and James Warner Björkman, eds. (1997). *Health Policy Reform, National Variations, and Globalization*. London: MacMillan Press Ltd.

Battle, Ken (1998). *Transformation: Canadian Social Policy, 1985–2001*. Victoria, BC: The North American Institute.

Belsky, J., and J. Casidy (1994). "Attachment: Theory and Evidence." In M. Rutter and D. Hay, eds., *Development through Life: A Handbook for Clinicians* (Oxford: Blackwell Scientific Publications): 549–71.

Bibby, Reginald W. (2004). *The Future Families Project: A Survey of Canadian Hopes and Dreams*. Section 5, "Parenting and Parents." Ottawa, ON: The Vanier Institute of the Family.

Bishop, John (1999). "How Provincial Diploma Exams Improve Student Learning." *Fraser Forum* (September). Vancouver: The Fraser Institute.

Blank, Rebecca M., and P. Ruggles (1994). "Short-Term Recidivism among Public-Assistance Recipients." *American Economic Review* 84, 2: 49–53.

Boessenkool, Kenneth J. (1997). *Back to Work: Learning from the Alberta Welfare Experiment*. C.D. Howe Institute Commentary (April). Toronto: C.D. Howe Institute.

Bosetti, L., R. O'Reilly, and D. Gereluk (1998). "Public Choices and Public Education: The Impact of Alberta Charter Schools." Paper presented at the Annual Meeting of the American Educational Research Association, San Diego, CA.

British Columbia Ministry of Human Resources, Economic Analysis Branch (2003). *MHR Exit Survey—Winter 2003*. Digital document available at http://www.mhr.gov.bc.ca/research/reports/MHR_Q4.pdf (October 2003).

Burchinal, Margaret R. (1999). "Child Care Experiences and Developmental Outcomes." *Annals of American Academy of Political Science* 563 (May): 73–97.

Bussière, Patrick, Fernando Cartwright, Tamara Knighto (2004). *Measuring Up: Canadian Results of the OECD PISA Study—The Performance of Canada's Youth in Mathematics, Reading, Science and Problem Solving: 2003 First Findings for Canadians Aged 15*. Ottawa: Minister of Industry.

Canada Council on Social Development [CCSD] (2004). *Child Care for a Change!* Conference Proceedings. Winnipeg, MB (November 12-14, 2004). Available online at http://www.ccsd.ca/subsites/child care/cc-proceedings.pdf.

Canadian Press/Leger Marketing (2003). *Canadians and Back to School*. August 25. Montreal.

Cao, Jian (1996). *Welfare Recipiency and Welfare Recidivism: An Analysis of the NLSY Data*. Madison, WI: Institute for Research on Poverty.

Cleverley, William O., and Roger K. Harvey (1992). "Is There a Link between Hospital Profit and Quality?" *Health Care Financial Management* (September) 46, 9: 40, 42, 44–45.

Commission d'étude sur les services de santé et les services sociaux (2001). *Les Solutions Émergentes*. Québec: Gouvernement du Québec. Digital document available at *http://www.cessss.gouv.qc.ca/pdf/ fr/00-109.pdf* (July 7, 2003).

Compas (1998). "Canadian Public Opinion on Families and Public Policy." Report to Southam News and the National Foundation for Family Research and Education (NFFRE). November 23. Toronto, ON: Compas, Inc. Available online at http://www.fact.on.ca/compas/compas.htm.

Compas (2003). "Ontario Provincial Election Report for Global TV, National Post, Ottawa Citizen and Windsor Star." May 29. Toronto, ON: Compas, Inc. Available online at http://www.compas.ca/data/030521-GlobalOnProvElection-E.pdf.

Council of Ministers of Education, Canada [CMEC] (2005). [Website] http://www.cmec.ca/index.en.html.

Currie, Janet, and Duncan Thomas (1997). "Do the Benefits of Early Childhood Education Last?" *Policy Options* (July-Aug).

DiLorenzo, Thomas J. (1984). *The Myth of Government Job Creation*. Policy Analysis. Washington, DC: The Cato Institute. Digital document available at http://www.cato.org/pubs/pas/pa048es.html (October 2003).

Dodenhoff, David (1998). *Privatizing Welfare in Wisconsin: Ending Administrative Entitlements—W-2s Untold Story*. Thiensville, WI: Wisconsin Policy Research Institute.

Esmail, Nadeem, and Michael Walker (2005a). *Waiting Your Turn: Hospital Waiting Lists in Canada, 15ᵗʰ edition*. Vancouver: The Fraser Institute.

Esmail, Nadeem, and Michael Walker (2005b). *How Good is Canadian Health Care? 2005 Report*. Vancouver: The Fraser Institute.

Feachem, Richard G.A., Neelam K. Sekhri, and Karen L. White (2002). "Getting More for Their Dollar: A Comparison of the NHS with California's Kaiser Permanente." *British Medical Journal* 324: 135–41.

Ferguson, Brian S. (2002). *Profits and the Hospital Sector: What Does the Literature Really Say?* Halifax, NS: Atlantic Institute for Market Studies. <http://www.aims.ca/commentary/profits.pdf>.

Ferson, M.J. (1994). "Control of Infections in Child Care." *Medical Journal of Australia* 161: 615–18.

Frenette, M., and G. Picot (2003). *Life after Welfare: The Economic Well-Being of Welfare Leavers in Canada during the 1990s.* Analytical Studies Research Paper Series 192. Ottawa: Statistics Canada.

Friendly, Martha, and Jane Beach (2005). *Early Childhood Education and Care in Canada 2004.* Toronto: Child Care Resource and Research Unit (CCRU). Available online at www.child carecanada.org.

Gabel, Todd, Jason Clemens, and Sylvia LeRoy (2004). *Welfare Reform in Ontario: A Report Card.* Fraser Institute Digital Publication. Vancouver, BC: The Fraser Institute. Available at www.fraserinstitute.ca.

Gagné, Lynda G. (2003). *Parental Work, Child-Care Use and Young Children's Cognitive Outcomes.* Statistics Canada Catalogue No. 89-594-XIE. Ottawa: Ministry of Industry.

General Accounting Office [GAO] (1997). "Head Start: Research Provides Little Information on Impact of Current Program." Report to the Chairman, Committee on the Budget, House of Representatives (April). Available online at http://www.gao.gov/archive/1997/he97059.pdf.

Government of Canada (2004). *Tax Expenditures and Evaluations—2004.* Electronic document available on the Internet at http://www.fin.gc.ca/toce/2004/taxexp04_e.html.

Government of Canada (2005a). *Early Childhood Development Activities and Expenditures/Early Learning and Child Care Activities and Expenditures.* Ottawa, ON: Government of Canada. Available online at http://socialunion.gc.ca/ecd/2004/english/page00.html.

Government of Canada (2005b). *The Budget Plan 2005*. Ottawa: Department of Finance Canada. Available online at http://www.fin.gc.ca/budget05/pdf/bp2005e.pdf.

Government of Manitoba (2005a). "Moving Forward: Governments of Canada and Manitoba Sign an Agreement on Early Learning and Child Care." News Release (April 29). Available online at http://www.gov.mb.ca/chc/press/top/2005/04/2005-04-29-07.html.

Government of Manitoba (2005b). *Moving Forward on Early Learning and Child Care: Manitoba's Action Plan—Next Steps*. Winnipeg, MB: Government of Manitoba. Available online at http://www.gov.mb.ca/fs/childcare/moving_forward.html.

Government of Ontario, Office of the Provincial Auditor (2001). *2001 Annual Report*. VFM Section 3.06. Toronto: Queen's Printer for Ontario

Government of Quebec (1999). *La Ministère de la Famille et de l'Enfance. Rapport Annuel 1998–1999*. Saint Foy, QC: Les Publications du Quebec. Available online at http://www.mfacf.gouv.qc.ca/ministere/rapports_annuels_en.asp.

Government of Quebec (2004). *Public Accounts, 2003–2004. Volume 2*. Finances Quebec. Available online at http://www.finances.gouv.qc.ca/en/documents/publications/pdf/vol2-2003-2004.pdf.

Graham, John R. (2002). "Dead Capital on Ontario's Hospitals." *Fraser Forum* (April): 23–24.

Grogger, J., and C. Michalopoulos (2003). "Welfare Dynamics under Time Limits." *Journal of Political Economy* 3, 3: 530–53.

Hamilton, Gayle, S. Freedman, L. Gennetian, C. Michalopoulos, J. Walter, D. Adams-Ciardullo, and A. Gassman-Pines (2001). *National Evaluation of Welfare-to-Work Strategies: How Effective Are Different Welfare-to-Work Approaches? Five-Year Adult and Child Impacts for Eleven Programs*. Washington, DC: US Department of Health and Human Services, Administration for Children and Families, Office of the Assistant Secretary for Planning and Evaluation; US Department of Education, Office of the Under Secretary, Office of Vocational and Adult Education.

Harding, Lesley (1998). *Case Studies: America Works, USA* (May). Digital document available at http://www.sustainability.org.uk/info/casestudies/america.htm (October, 2003).

Hepburn, Claudia, and Robert Van Belle (unpublished). "Ten Case Studies of School Choice in Canada." Available from the author.

Hepburn, Claudia R., and Robert Van Belle (2003). *The Canadian Education Freedom Index*. Studies in Education Policy (September). Vancouver: The Fraser Institute.

Hoxby, Caroline M. (2001). "How School Choice Affects the Achievement of Public School Students." Paper prepared for the Koret Task Force meeting at the Hoover Institution, Stanford, CA (September 20–21, 2001). Available at http://post.economics.harvard.edu/faculty/hoxby/papers/choice_sep01.pdf.

Human Resources and Skills Development Canada [HRSDC] (1999). *1998 Employment Insurance Monitoring and Assessment Report*. Available at http://www.hrsdc.gc.ca/asp/gateway.asp?hr=en/ei/reports/eimar.shtml&hs=ada.

Human Resources and Skills Development Canada [HRSDC] (2000). *1999 Employment Insurance Monitoring and Assessment Report*. Available at http://www.hrsdc.gc.ca/asp/gateway.asp?hr=en/ei/reports/eimar.shtml&hs=ada.

Human Resources and Skills Development Canada [HRSDC] (2001). *2000 Employment Insurance Monitoring and Assessment Report.* Available at http://www.hrsdc.gc.ca/asp/gateway.asp?hr=en/ei/reports/eimar. shtml&hs=ada.

Human Resources and Skills Development Canada [HRSDC] (2002). *2001 Employment Insurance Monitoring and Assessment Report.* Available at http://www.hrsdc.gc.ca/asp/gateway.asp?hr=en/ei/reports/eimar. shtml&hs=ada.

Human Resources and Skills Development Canada [HRSDC] (2003). *2002 Employment Insurance Monitoring and Assessment Report.* Available at http://www.hrsdc.gc.ca/asp/gateway.asp?hr=en/ei/reports/eimar. shtml&hs=ada.

Human Resources and Skills Development Canada [HRSDC] (2004a). *2003 Employment Insurance Monitoring and Assessment Report.* Available at http://www.hrsdc.gc.ca/asp/gateway.asp?hr=en/ei/reports/eimar. shtml&hs=ada.

Human Resources and Skills Development Canada [HRSDC] (2004b). *Chief Actuary's Outlook on the Employment Insurance Account for 2005.* Batineau, QC: Actuarial Services HRSDC, October. Available online at http://www. hrsdc.gc.ca/en/ei/reports/pr2005.pdf.

Human Resources and Skills Development Canada [HRSDC] (2005). *2004 Employment Insurance Monitoring and Assessment Report.* Available online at http://www.hrsdc.gc.ca/asp/gateway.asp?hr=en/ei/reports/eimar. shtml&hs=ada.

Hsia, David C., and Cathaleen A. Ahern (1992). "Good quality care increases hospital profits under prospective payment." *Health Care Financing Review* Spring 13, 3: 17–24.

Lefebvre, Pierre (2004). "Quebec's Innovative Early Childhood Education and Care Policy and Its Weaknesses." *Policy Options* (March). Montreal: IRPP.

Lefebvre, Pierre, and Philip Merrigan (2002). "The Effect of Child Care and Early Education Arrangement on Developmental Outcomes of Young Children." *Canadian Public Policy* 28, 2 (June): 159–86.

Lefebvre, Pierre, and Philip Merrigan (2003). *Assessing Family Policy in Canada*. IRPP Choices 9, 5 (June).

Magnuson, Katherine A., Christopher J. Ruhm, and Jane Waldfogel (2004). *Does Prekindergarten Improve School Preparation and Performance?* NBER Working Paper 10452 (April). Cambridge, MA: National Bureau of Economic Research. Available online at http://www.nber.org/papers/w10452.

McArthur, William (1996). "Private Hospitals Improve Public Sector Health Care." *Fraser Forum* (December): 24–26.

McKey, Ruth, et al. (1985). "The Impact of Head Start on Children, Families, and Communities." HHS 85-31193 (June). US Department of Health and Human Services.

Megginson, William L., and Jeffery M. Netter (2001). "From State to Market: A Survey of Empirical Studies on Privatization." *Journal of Economic Literature* 39, 2: 321–89.

Meyer, Daniel R., and M. Cancian (1996). "Life after Welfare." *Public Welfare* 54: 25–29.

Michalski, Joseph H. (1999). "Values and Preferences for the 'Best Policy Mix' for Canadian Children." CPRN Discussion Paper No. F/05 (May).

Mihlar, F., and D. Smith (1997). *Government-Sponsored Training Programs: Failure in the United States, Lessons for Canada.* Critical Issues Bulletin (December). Vancouver, BC: The Fraser Institute.

Ministry of Community and Social Services [MCSS], Government of Ontario (1999). *Government's Private Sector Initiative Creates New Jobs for Ontario Works Participants in Sudbury.* News Release (March 15). Toronto: Communications and Marketing Branch.

Ministry of Community, Family, and Children's Services [MCFCS], Government of Ontario (2000). *Zero Tolerance for Welfare Fraud.* Backgrounder (January 18).

Ministry of Community, Family, and Children's Services [MCFCS], Government of Ontario (2001). Ontario Works Policy Directives, September 2001. Digital document available at http://www.cfcs.gov.on.ca/CFCS/en/programs/IES/OntarioWorks/Publications/ow-policydirectives.htm (October 2003).

Moon, Rachel T. (2000). "Sudden Infant Death Syndrome in Child Care Settings." *Pediatrics* 106: 295–300.

National Center for Policy Analysis (2000). *Idea House.* Digital document available at http://www.ncpa.org/hotlines/juvcrm/d2.html (October 2003).

National Council of Welfare [NCW] (2004). *Fact Sheet: Welfare Recipients.* Digital document available at http://www.ncwcnbes.net/htmdocument/principales/numberwelfare_e.htm.

National Council of Welfare [NCW] (2005). *Welfare Incomes 2004.* Digital document available at http://www.ncwcnbes.net/htmdocument/report-WelfareIncomes2004/WI2004EngREVISED.pdf.

New, Michael J. (2002). *Welfare Reform That Works: Explaining the Welfare Caseload Decline, 1996–2000*. Washington, DC: The Cato Institute.

New York State Department of Labor (1997). "Memorandum from Pete Landsberg to John Haley" (June 11, 1997).

NICHD Early Child Care Research Network (1996). "Characteristics of Infant Child Care: Factors Contributing to Positive Caregiving." *Early Childhood Research Quarterly* 11: 269–306.

NICHD Early Child Care Research Network (2003). "Does Amount of Time Spent in Child Care Predict Socioemotional Adjustment During the Transition to Kindergarten?" *Child Development* 74, 4: 976–1005.

Olsen, Darcy Ann (2005). "Is Preschool Good for Children?" *Fraser Forum* (May): 5–6.

Ontario Regulation 134/98. Ontario Works Act, 1997. Digital Document available at http://www.cfcs.gov.on.ca/CFCS/en/programs/IES/OntarioWorks/Legislation/default.htm.

Organisation for Economic Cooperation and Development [OECD] (2001). *Education at a Glance*. Paris: OECD

Ouchi, William (2004). "Academic Freedom." *Education Next* (Winter). Available online at http://www.educationnext.org/2004/21.html.

Pauly, Mark V. (1968). "The Economics of Moral Hazard: Comment." *The American Economic Review* 58: 531–37.

Rector, Robert (1997). *Wisconsin's Welfare Miracle*. Digital document available at http://www.heritage.org/Research/Welfare/index.cfm (October 2003).

Rector, R., and S. Youssef (1999). *The Determinants of Welfare Caseload Decline.* Washington, DC: The Heritage Foundation.

Reidl, B., and R. Rector (2002). *Myths and Facts: Why Successful Welfare Reform Must Strengthen Work Requirements.* Washington, DC: The Heritage Foundation.

Rhoads, Steven E. (2004). *Taking Sex Differences Seriously.* San Francisco, CA: Encounter Books.

Rooney, Jennifer, Donna Lero, Karen Korabik, and Denise L. Whitehead (2003). *Self-Employment for Women: Policy Options that Promote Equality and Economic Opportunities.* Ottawa: Status of Women Canada.

Rutter, Michael (1995). "Clinical Implications of Attachment Concepts: Retrospect and Prospect." *Journal of Child Psychological Psychiatry* 36: 549–71.

Schafer, Chris, Joel Emes, and Jason Clemens (2001). *Surveying US and Canadian Welfare Reform.* Critical Issues Bulletin. Vancouver, BC: The Fraser Institute.

Stafford, Janine (2002). *A Profile of the Child Care Services Industry.* Catalogue No. 63-016-XPB (September). Ottawa: Ministry of Industry, Statistics Canada, Service Industries Division.

Statistics Canada (2001). "Trends in the Use of Private Education." *The Daily* (July 4). Available digitally at www.statcan.ca/Daily/English/010704/d010704.pdf.

Statistics Canada (2004). "Employment Insurance Coverage Survey." *The Daily* (June 22). Available online at http://www.statcan.ca/Daily/English/040622/d040622c.htm.

Statistics Canada (2005a). *Annual Demographic Statistics*. Catalogue No. 91-213-XIB (March 31).

Statistics Canada (2005b). "Child Care." *The Daily* (February 7). Available online at http://www.statcan.ca/Daily/English/050207/d050207b.htm.

Statistics Canada (2005c). "Employment Insurance Coverage Survey." *The Daily* (June 22). Available online at http://www.statcan.ca/Daily/English/050622/d050622d.htm.

Statistics Canada (2005d). *Provincial Economic Accounts* 1981–2004.

Statistics Canada, Public Institutions Division (2005). Financial Management System. Ottawa, ON: Statistics Canada.

Strategic Council (2002). "A Family Snapshot: Canadian Attitudes on the Family." Vancouver, BC: Focus on the Family Canada.

Tomal, Annette (1998). "The Relationship between Hospital Mortality Rates, and Hospital, Market and Patient Characteristics." *Applied Economics* 30: 717–25.

United Nations. *United Nations Declaration of Human Rights*, Article 26.

United States Department of Health and Human Services, The Administration for Children and Families [USHHS] (2003). *Temporary Assistance for Needy Families Program (TANF): Fifth Annual Report to Congress*. Washington, DC: United States Department of Health and Human Services, February. Also available as a digital document http://www.acf.dhhs.gov/programs/ofa/annualreport5/ (October 2003).

United States General Accounting Office [USGAO] (1978). *Job Training Programs Need More Effective Management*. Washington, DC: United States General Accounting Office.

United States General Accounting Office [USGAO] (1979). *Moving Participants from Public Service Programs into Unsubsidized Jobs Needs More Attention*. Washington, DC: United States General Accounting Office.

United States General Accounting Office [USGAO] (1980). *Labor Should Make Sure CETA Programs Have Effective Employability Development Systems*. Washington, DC: United States General Accounting Office.

Veldhuis, Niels, and Jason Clemens (2004). "Does Canada Have a Marriage Tax Penalty?" *Fraser Forum* (March).

Windsor Star (2005). "Split Decision on Child Care." *Windsor Star* (February 12): A9.

Wößmann, Ludgar (2000). *Schooling Resources, Educational Institutions, and Student Performance: The International Evidence*. Kiel Working Paper No. 983. Keil, Germany: The Kiel Institute of World Economics.

Zelder, Martin (2000). *How Private Hospital Competition Can Improve Canadian Healthcare*. Public Policy Source 35. Vancouver, BC: The Fraser Institute.

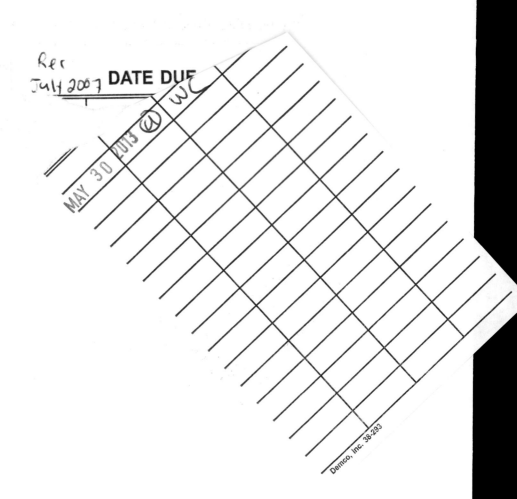